The Queer Cookbook

The Queer Cookbook

**A Fully-guided Tour to the Secrets of Success
in the Homosexual Kitchen!**

Compiled by Donna Clark

Illustrated by David Shenton

FREEDOM EDITIONS

For a catalogue of related titles in our Contemporary Studies
publishing programme please write to us at the address below:

Cassell
Wellington House
125 Strand
London WC2R 0BB

PO Box 605
Herndon
VA 20172

First published 1997

British Library Cataloguing-in-Publication Data
A catalogue record for this book is available from the British
Library.

ISBN: 0 304 33812 5

Printed and bound in Great Britain by
Biddles Ltd, Guildford and King's Lynn

FOR CHRISTOPHER WINTER

Contents

Introduction

Why a queer cookbook?
It's true that queers are into cuisine. As a litmus test I casually asked a random selection of homosexuals whether they could cook. They all replied instantly that not only could they cook, but they were probably the best cook, party host and all-round entertainer that they knew. This book puts that to the test.

What makes a queer recipe?
Simple, a recipe that's been made for or by a queer.

What's in the book?
A vast, eclectic, sumptuous mêlée of dishes from queers I've met and queers on the Internet. Plus all those handy hints and tips to make your mealtimes and catering adventures go with a bang.

Conversion etc.
The recipes may be approximate because few people seem to continue measuring after they've made the recipe several times, therefore many of my contributors used *helpful* measurements like 'some' or 'a bit' or 'a lump of' and so forth, so my suggestion is that you try them out with an open mind and adjust to your own tastes.

The recipes come from both the UK and the US, and the measurements vary, as Americans measure in volume and Europeans measure in weight. They're all pretty straightforward, though, and I wouldn't want to alter a recipe that I've been given. The following conversion lists should help.

To convert

Ounces to Grams multiply by 30
Pounds to Kilograms multiply by 0.48
Teaspoons to Millilitres multiply by 5
Tablespoons to Millilitres multiply by 15
Imperial Pints to Litres multiply by 0.50
Cups to Litres multiply by 0.25
Inches to Centimetres multiply by 2.5

Temperatures

130°C	250°F	Gas Mark ½
140°C	275°F	Gas Mark 1
150°C	300°F	Gas Mark 2
170°C / 160°C	325°F	Gas Mark 3
180°C	350°F	Gas Mark 4
190°C	375°F	Gas Mark 5
200°C	400°F	Gas Mark 6
220°C / 210°C	425°F	Gas Mark 7
230°C	450°F	Gas Mark 8

Weights

30 g = 1 oz	350 g = 12 oz	225 g = 8 oz
85 g = 3 oz	55 g = 2 oz	450 g = 1 lb
140 g = 5 oz	110 g = 4 oz	1 kg = 2.25 lb
200 g = 7 oz	170 g = 6 oz	

Vegetables

Root vegetables, chopped 1 lb = 3 cups
Onions, sliced or chopped 1 lb = 3 cups
Potatoes 1 lb = 3 cups
Spinach or other greens
(cooked and chopped) 1 lb = 1½ cups

Liquid and Dry Measures

a pinch = slightly less than ⅛ teaspoon
a dash = a few drops
3 teaspoons = 1 tablespoon
2 tablespoons = 1 fluid ounce
2 British tablespoons = 2-3 American tablespoons
4 tablespoons = ½ cup
2 cups = 1 pint

An Imperial/American Guide to solid and liquid measures

Imperial	American	Imperial	American
Solid measures		Liquid measures	
1 lb butter or margarine	2 cups	¼ pint liquid	⅔ cup liquid
1 lb flour	4 cups	½ pint	1¼ cups
1 lb granulated or		¾ pint	2 cups
caster sugar	2 cups	1 pint	2½ cups
1 lb icing sugar	3 cups	1½ pints	3¾ cups
8 oz rice	1 cup	2 pints	5 cups (2½ pints)

British Terms – American Terms
Ingredients UK – US

aubergine – eggplant
bicarbonate of soda – baking soda
caster sugar – superfine sugar
cornflour – cornstarch
courgette – zucchini
digestive biscuits – graham crackers
double cream – heavy cream
icing sugar – confectioner's sugar
mangetout – snow peas

plain chocolate – semi-sweet chocolate
plain flour – all purpose flour
self-raising flour –
flour sifted with baking powder
shortcrust pastry – basic pie dough
single cream – light cream
spring onion – scallion
sultanas – golden raisins
tomato purée – tomato paste

Other terms
frying pan – skillet
baking tray – baking or cookie sheet
greaseproof paper – waxed paper
grill – broil
Swiss-roll tin – jelly roll pan

Note
All recipes that **derive from the US**, and to
which US measurements and terms should therefore
apply, are marked with this sign.

Recipes particularly suitable for vegetarians have (**v**) in brackets after
the name.

Etiquette
Queer culinary tips

Always wait until the boys have retired to the drawing room before handing round the port and cigars.

1. The Dinner Guest

• Always compliment the chef, even if the food tastes terrible.

• Bring two bottles of wine (even if you don't drink) – one fairly good and one average. Don't mention the disparity but firmly advise opening the good one first. By the time you get to the second, the party will be less discerning.

• Arrive late, but not too late. Most culinary queer geniuses will underestimate preparation time, but if the food's charred you'll be the one who's to blame.

• Avoid condiments. Excessive salt and peppering can be seen as insulting, as the chef may have delicate, if bland, sensibilities.

• Test the water for smoke tolerance. If you smoke and no one else seems to be lighting up, take a deep (smoke-free) breath, grin and bear it.

• Stay late (unless your hosts are comatose). A dinner party's success

is often gauged upon the time it ends, so don't insult your entertainers by leaving early to watch *Eurotrash* or catch last orders.
• Don't get caught snooping around the bedrooms. If you do, make up an extremely plausible excuse like 'just looking for the loo' or at a push 'did you get the idea for your colour schemes from *Elle Decoration* or are you naturally hugely visually creative?'
• Don't drink before you arrive, there's nothing worse than wasted guests oophing down your meticulously crafted canapés.
• Save yourself for the main course. Queers do have a tendency to overestimate appetites, and a little of everything is preferable to three bowls of soup, four bread rolls and no room for anything else.
• Wash before you arrive. Personal hygiene is extremely important at a culinary event.

2.Tips for the host

• Never run out of alcohol – a dry party is a no-no for your average boozing homos.
• Presentation is always key. Wash the cutlery, tablecloths and serving gloves – no self-respecting homosexual wants to eat with soiled apparatus.
• Modesty is very important. You must strike a delicate balance between 'oh, it took no time at all' and 'I've been rouxing since Thursday last'.
• Don't mention Delia.
• Always make a sweet. Even if it's three bananas and a jug of cream, it gives the impression of a fully balanced menu.
• Don't leave stock-cube wrappers, sauce-mix packets and ready-trimmed vegetable packaging lying around. Instead a well-thumbed Elizabeth David can make all the difference.
• Don't be too adventurous if you've invited a delicate mix of strangers and acquaintances. Something that could be humorously disastrous to you and your lover will seem embarrassingly burnt to your guests.
• Use dimmer switches and candles to disguise unappealing food and crockery.
• Use colour to liven up a bland meal. I'm not saying that homosexuals can be superficial but attention to detail is essential, and 'batons' sound so much more appetizing than 'chunks'.
• If you're going to use words like 'coulis' or 'flambé', learn how to pronounce them first.

3. Selection of Guests

• Avoid ex-lovers at all costs.
• Be mindful of political persuasions. A gay Conservative and a queer radical will potentially not only fight but be hugely irritating and boring to the rest of your party.
• Twelve-steppers and in-denial alchoholics don't mix.
• Sit next to the quietest ones (unless you're painfully quiet yourself). Don't leave them alone gazing melancholically into their soups at the the end of the table.
• Don't invite a selection of your ex-college friends and your new lover. The conversation will inevitably plummet to the depths of flatulence and yard-of-ale reminiscences.
• Hardened carnivores and strict vegetarians are not particularly compatible, unless you're prepared to cook one menu for each group.

4. Tips For The Perfect Kitsch Kitchen

• You can't go wrong with Sabatier knives and Le Creuset. They're worth the investment in my opinion, as is a food processor.
• If a partner or friend owes you a 'serious favour' and foolishly says 'I'll do anything', make them clean the fridge.
• Although the idea of open shelving in kitchens is pretty cool and has been tempting all of us from the pages of style magazines, you can only really get away with it if you've got the crockery to match. Cupboards are extremely useful for hiding crap floral plates and mugs.
• Have two lighting arrangements. Fluorescent strips or bright ceiling lights may stop you cutting your fingers to bits but are never flattering, so switch if guests arrive.
• If you've got friends coming round for dinner, do all the dull preparation before they arrive, so that they only see you tweaking your creation, tasting and seasoning, as opposed to peeling which can be less than glamorous.
• You can't have too many kitchen utensils.
• An essential implement is a pasta grabber – it can make all the difference. Tongs can also be indispensable for picking up things you'd rather not handle.
• Industrial rubber gloves are not only practical, but bizarrely sexy.

5. Ins and outs of the kitsch kitchen

o u t s
pasta jars (no, no, no)
coffee percolators (just the word 'percolator' says it all)
Schwartz spice racks
jars of pulses
all-colour cookbooks
electric juicers

i n s
griddle pans
amaretti boxes
Teasmades
fresh herbs
wire pan-racks
Fanny Craddock
Soda Streams

Queer foodstuffs

o u t s
organic baked beans
veggie burgers
Quorn
mixed herbs (especially basil)
herbal teas
decaff
fresh pasta (waste of money, if you ask me)
baby vegetables

i n s
Alphabetti-spaghetti
sausages
fresh herbs
Tetley's
Lavazza expresso
dried pasta (the authentic original)
root vegetables

Breakfast

Lesbian, Gay, Bisexual & Transgendered Pride Breakfast

Serves anyone who identifies
as hungry

A Pride breakfast is a must for the culinary queer calender, it peps you up for the day's events and starts Pride with a bang (or a pop depending on the quality of the sparkling wine). Not the most energetic of breakfasts but lets face it if you've got several hours of marching, blowing whistles, listening to naff acts you'd forgotten existed, drinking warm beer and avoiding all the people you've stood up in the last year, you won't want to be up to your armpits in washing up when you finally stagger home.

Ingredients
1 bottle of pink Cava (obviously if you're rich you'll go for the real stuff but Cava will do)
1 punnet of strawberries
croissants
fromage frais (or cream)
orange juice

Method
Wash the strawberries and take the cores out (I know it's a pain but your homosexuals, bisexuals, transsexuals and friendly heterosexual's will appreciate the effort). Pop the croissants in a medium oven. Arrange your fare artistically, pour on the cream (or fromage frais for the health conscious) and crack open the bubbly.

Hangover Breakfast

Serves 2

The best thing for a hangover is a massive fry-up. Although it's tempting to go to the nearest greasy spoon/diner, fry-ups can actually be a skilled exercise in fat consumption. The options are endless – ranging from scrambled eggs, to bubble and squeak, and eggy bread. But the classic hangover breakfast is:

Ingredients

2 lbs potatoes
sunflower oil
paprika
cayenne pepper
4 rashers bacon
4 pork sausages
½ lb mushrooms
knob of butter
4 tomatoes
1 tin Heinz baked beans (and only Heinz will do)
2 eggs
sour cream (optional)

Method

Peel the potatoes and chop into 1 inch pieces. Blanch them in water for five minutes until they're slightly fluffy at the edges, then drain. Heat some oil in a frying pan and add the potatoes. Sprinkle liberally with paprika and cautiously with cayenne and fry, regularly turning them. At this stage, pop the bacon and sausages under the grill. Wash and chop the mushrooms and fry them with a knob of butter in a saucepan, then pop the halved tomatoes under the grill. Ten minutes later, heat the beans through, fry the eggs and serve the whole enormous amount. You can serve the home-fries with sour cream if you want.

Ease the passage of the food with a large pot of tea (none of your Earl Grey nonsense, just plain old Tetley's will do).

Eggs Benedict
Serves 6

Ingredients
3 English muffins
6 slices broiled ham or Canadian bacon
6 poached eggs
asparagus (optional)
hollandaise sauce

Method
Split and toast the English muffins (white rolls or baps will do). Cut the ham or bacon to the same size as the muffins; place on the muffins. Slip an egg on top of the ham. Add asparagus (if liked) and cover with hollandaise sauce. Serve hot.

Tip
**For variation on the same theme:
Add asparagus spears between ham and egg layers. Add slices of broiled tomato between egg and ham, and serve with cheese sauce (sometimes this is called 'Eggs Robin Hood', God only knows why)**

To Make the Hollandaise Sauce

Ingredients
½ cup butter
2 egg yolks, well beaten
1 dash cayenne pepper
1 tablespoon lemon juice
¼ teaspoon salt
½ cup boiling water

Method
Take your trusty food processor and cream the butter and add the egg yolks one at a time, blending each one in thoroughly. Add the remaining ingredients and blend. Just before serving, add ½ cup boiling water gradually, beating constantly. Cook over hot water, stirring constantly, until thickened. Serve at once.

Tip
If the mixture curdles, whisk in a teaspoon of boiling water a drop at a time. If that doesn't work, put an egg yolk in a bowl and add this slowly to the sauce, beating with a whisk.

K e d g e r e e
Serves 4–6

A classic breakfast dish.

Ingredients
1 lb smoked cod or haddock
bay leaf
2 oz butter
1 small onion, finely chopped
1 teaspoon ground cumin
1 teaspoon ground coriander
½ teaspoon turmeric
8 oz long grain rice
½ pint single cream
2 or 3 hard-boiled eggs,
quartered

M e t h o d

Poach the fish in water with the bay leaf. Remove the fish (saving the liquid). Flake the white flesh of the fish, taking away the skin and removing the bones. Strain the poaching liquid and make up to one pint.

In a large saucepan, melt the butter and fry the onion until soft. Add the spices and continue frying, stirring quickly for a minute. Stir in the rice. Add the poaching liquid and bring to the boil. Cover and simmer for 20 minutes until the rice is cooked. Add the fish and toss gently.

Meanwhile, warm the cream over a gentle heat. Taste the rice to check the seasoning, adjust to taste, then place the rice mixture on a warmed serving dish. Pour the cream over the rice and arrange the eggs on the top.

T i p
If you've got any of the fish liquid left over, save it and use as soup stock.

Bubble and Squeak
Serves 6

When you're ravenously hung-over, this is the perfect antidote.

Ingredients

1 tablespoon bacon fat, lard or oil

1 small onion, chopped

1½ lb mashed potato

8 oz cold cooked savoy cabbage

salt and pepper

tomato ketchup to serve

Method
Melt the fat in a pan and fry the onion until it's transparent. Add the potato and cabbage, stirring in to break up the lumps. Season well with salt and pepper and continue to fry over a medium heat until the sides are crispy brown. Keep turning the potato and cabbage, being careful not to burn them, but ensuring that all the sides are coated and crispy. Serve with oodles of tomato ketchup.

Tip

You can use blanched potatoes if you've got the patience but mashed is easier. The best thing about bubble and squeak is the crispiness so don't rush and burn your lovely brekkie.

Quentin Crisp's Scrambled Eggs for One

Ingredients

2 eggs

splash milk

2 slices white bread (nothing kinky like rye bread)

Method
Mix the eggs in whatever you have lying around. Add in some milk. Pour into a saucepan (I don't really bother to wash them before). Whisk with an old fork and stir until they're done, then put on the bread.

Bert Tyler-Moore's Special Brunch

This is very much a Sunday at home with your boyfriend or girlfriend. Ideal for eating whilst reading the papers and before going to see some films.

Poached Eggs à la Bert

Ingredients
granary bread
2 eggs per person
1 packet spinach
handful grated mature
Cheddar cheese
1 packet shaved ham

Method

Toast the granary bread, poach the eggs and boil the spinach. On one piece of toast, place some spinach and a handful of grated cheese, then put one of the poached eggs on top. On the other piece, put some shaved ham (enough to cover the bread) and a handful of cheese, and put the other egg on that piece.

Tip

Even easier than boiling the spinach, you can now get spinach in microwave bags for extra ease and the spinach comes out crunchier and less soggy.

Yoggy Muesli Surprise
Serves 1

Ingredients
pot of vanilla yogurt
dessertspoonful crème fraîche
banana
Swiss-style muesli

Method
Put the yoghurt and crème fraîche into your dessert bowl. Chop the banana on the top of them and sprinkle the Swiss-style muesli over the top.

Fish's Creative Croissants
Serves 2

After that late night when you're still trying to impress your new partner, this is the ideal breakfast. It does help if you happen to live near the Di Lieto bakery in Stockwell, but any bakery will probably do.

Ingredients
2 croissants
2 oz medium Cheddar cheese, grated
4 tablespoons mayonnaise
1 teaspoon English mustard
2 tomatoes, sliced
fresh salad and orange juice, to serve

Serving
Send the girlfriend out to the bakery for the croissants – this enables you to dress and clean your teeth. Mix the mayonnaise and mustard in a bowl. When the girlfriend arrives back with the croissants, put them in a medium oven (Gas Mark 3 or 4). When slightly warmed, take the croissants out of the oven and cut them in half; put the cheese on the bottom. Pour over the mayonnaise and mustard mix, and a sliced tomato. Pop them back into the oven for 5 – 10 minutes and serve with a nice fresh salad and a glass of fresh orange juice.

Soups and

Starters

Henry Collier's Corn Chowder
Serves 2 – 3

Henry is the treasurer of the Sydney Gay and Lesbian Rights Lobby, and a Senior Lecturer in the Department of Accounting and Finance at the University of Wollongong in Australia. This recipe is especially for his partner, Kim Yoon Ho.

Ingredients

8 oz chopped bacon

1 tablespoon vegetable oil

1 clove garlic, chopped

1 medium/large onion, chopped

2 large potatoes
(cut into ½-inch cubes)

1½ cups water

1 x 16 oz can sweetcorn

1 x 16 oz can
creamed sweetcorn

8 oz heavy (double)
cream

black pepper to taste

Tip
Take your time ... simmer slowly ... like relationships, it takes a little time for the flavour to develop.

Method

First sauté the bacon for about 5 minutes in a large pan over a low heat. Let the bacon soften and begin to release the oils and fats. If you wish, you may drain the oil after the bacon has cooked. Add the garlic and the onion, and continue to cook over a low heat until the onions begin to brown. Add the potatoes and the water. Bring to the boil, then simmer for about 10 – 15 minutes over a low heat. The potatoes should be soft.

Add the corn and the creamed corn to the mixture and return to simmering point. If you wish, add more water to reach the desired consistency.

Before serving, remove from the heat. Add heavy cream. Reheat to serving temperature. Watch carefully, for if you boil the chowder, it may curdle. While this doesn't hurt the taste, the soup/chowder looks better when it is not separated.

Add black pepper to taste.

Donna's Healthy Lesbian Tomato and Lentil Soup (v)

Serves two hungry dykes

Ingredients

1 medium onion, finely chopped

1 tablespoon olive oil

2 cloves garlic

1 x 14 oz tin of tomatoes (chopped) or fresh tomatoes (skinned and chopped) if you happen to have them lying around

1 cup lentils

one pint vegetable stock

fresh parsley

2 oz Cheshire cheese (optional)

fresh wholemeal bread and a cup of tea, to serve

This thick and warming soup is perfect for those winter lunches when you can't quite be bothered to go out, and your food cupboard only contains a few lentils and a tin of tomatoes.

Method

Heat the oil, then fry the onion and the garlic in a large saucepan until the onion becomes transparent. Stir in the tomatoes and lentils. Add the stock, stir and bring to the boil. Simmer for 30 minutes with the lid on, stirring occasionally to stop the lentils from sticking to the bottom of the pan. Chop the parsley and add to the mixture. Cut the Cheshire cheese into small cubes and add a few minutes before serving (so that the outside of the cheese cubes are softened).

Serve with fresh wholemeal bread and a cup of tea.

Tip

There can be something overly hippy about lentils, but if you cook them for long enough, they disintegrate into a soothing, sumptuous, pulp which is totally appetising.

Claire's Spinach Soup (v)
Serves 4

Ingredients
1 medium onion
1 – 4 medium potatoes
depending on how thick
you like your soup. (I tried it
first with one potato but I
live with an Irish woman
and now use four potatoes
which she likes better.)
sunflower oil
½ lb to 1 lb frozen spinach
1½ pints vegetable stock
(bouillon is best)
pinch of nutmeg
juice of ½ lemon
salt and pepper

This recipe is brilliant because it takes no time at all: when you go to the supermarket you buy loads of frozen spinach, shove it away in your freezer and forget about it. When unheralded guests are coming, you're prepared.

Method
Cut up the onion and fry it in oil in a large saucepan, then slice your potatoes into inch-thick pieces and fry them in the oil. Add anywhere between half a pound to a pound of frozen spinach and stir. Then add in your vegetable stock, cover and boil for 20 minutes. Blend the soup and add a pinch of nutmeg and the lemon juice.

Serve seasoned with salt and pepper.

This is a good starter if you use one potato, and an excellent main course if you use four. It's also a brilliant green colour.

Potato and Leek Soup
(or Vichyssoise if you're posh) (v)
Serves 4

This really is the most superb soup for a cold winter's evening. It warms and satisfies.

Ingredients
2 oz butter
1 lb leeks, sliced
1½ lb potatoes,
cut into 1-inch cubes
2 pints vegetable stock
salt and pepper
½ pint double cream
chopped chives (optional)

Method
Melt the butter in a large pan and sweat the leeks for about 5 minutes. Add the potatoes (I keep the skin on them, I think it adds texture) and cook, stirring for about 3 or 4 minutes until basted with the butter. Add the stock, salt and pepper and bring to the boil. Cover the pan and simmer over a low flame until the potatoes are cooked (about 20 minutes). Remove from the heat, then stir in the cream when the potatoes are very fluffy and soft. Serve piping hot. Most makers of vichyssoise liquidise it, but I think that lessens the effect as the textures are so integral to the taste. Serve sprinkled with chopped chives, if liked.

Tip
If you are going to make this soup, thoroughly wash the leeks – there's nothing worse than crunching through dirt and it's also embarrassing. Slice the leeks from the top down to about halfway and flare out the leaves; this should enable you to remove all the dirt without losing too much of the veg-

Carrot, Orange and Coriander Soup (v)

Serves 4

Simple but effective.

Ingredients

2 large onions, chopped
2 oz butter
1 lb carrots, sliced
¼ pint fresh orange juice
salt and pepper
2 pints light vegetable stock
2 tablespoons fresh coriander, chopped
¼ pint sour cream

Method

Melt the butter in a pan and fry the onions until they're soft but not coloured. Add the carrots and fry for a further 5 minutes. Now pour in the orange juice and season with some salt and pepper. Cover the pan and simmer the soup for about 20 minutes or until the carrots are soft. Pour the soup into a liquidizer and blend until smooth. Add the stock and check the seasoning, then stir in half the chopped coriander. Simmer for 5 minutes. Then beat in the cream until the consistency is smooth. Serve garnished with the remaining chopped coriander

Tip

Soup looks at its best when it's garnished, so save back some of the cream and swirl it over the top of the bowls. Also, a lazy friend of mine (who shall remain nameless) used to just buy the cartons of carrot and coriander soup, add some more carrots, a bit of coriander and pretend she'd made it herself! I think I'm the only one who noticed, so it could be worth a stab if you're pushed for time.

Annie's Soup (v)
Serves 4

I made this once for a girl who used to go to school with my sister and since then it's been called 'Annie's Soup' after me.

Ingredients
3 – 5 onions, sliced into rings

½ lb mushrooms, sliced

2 medium potatoes, sliced into inch chunks

soy sauce

1½ pints vegetable stock

pinch of chilli powder

2 tablespoons fresh dill (chopped)

tablespoon white wine vinegar

salt and pepper

Greek yogurt (optional)

Method
Gently fry the onions and the mushrooms. Then add the potatoes and continue to fry. Add a dash of soy sauce so that the mixture doesn't stick. Next, add the stock, the chilli powder and the dill. Put the lid on the pan and cook for half an hour or until the potatoes are soft. Remove the lid and add the white wine vinegar (for a while your house will smell like a pickle factory) and adjust the seasoning to taste.

Serve with greek yougurt. Just put a tablespoon of Greek yogurt in each of the bowls and stir in – it's delicious.

Gazpacho (v)

Ingredients
1½ kg tomatoes
¾ teaspoon Worcestershire sauce
¾ teaspoon Tabasco sauce
1 clove garlic (optional)
2 teaspoons sugar
salt to taste
1 red pepper, finely chopped
1 large onion, finely chopped
1 cucumber, finely chopped
1 tomato, finely chopped

'Cold tomatoey soup' never sounds quite as delicious as Gazpacho actually is – a must for summer evenings.

Serves four hot chicks

Method
Place the tomatoes in boiling water for 10 minutes. Remove the skins and finely chop. Blend the tomatoes in a liquidizer and strain. Add the Worcestershire sauce, Tabasco sauce, garlic, sugar and salt. Chill thoroughly. Serve, sprinkled with chopped onion, cucumber and tomato, in cold bowls to hot guests.

Parsnip and Orange Soup (v)
Serves 4

This thick, sumptuous soup is warming, filling and delicious. I've served it to friends at dinner parties who've raved about it, and to family who've been extremely impressed at the fact that I can actually cook sensible food which isn't totally bland. You need a food processor and no amount of mashing will compensate for the lack of one, but the extra washing up is most definitely worth it.

Ingredients
1 lb parsnips
1 medium onion
1 oz butter (or olive oil)
2 pints vegetable stock (cubes will do)
2 oz curd cheese
zest of one orange, grated

Method

Peel and core the parsnips. (The core is the unpleasant part of the parsnip and has a bitter taste, so don't skimp on coring even though it's a complete pain in the arse and you'll probably remove layers of skin and some nails doing it. A girlfriend of mine even bought me a corer for Christmas one year because she loved this soup so much – it helps, but basically coring is hard, time-consuming work.

Slice the peeled, cored parsnips and finely chop the onion. Then melt the butter in a large saucepan and sweat the parsnips and onion for 10 minutes. When the parsnips are looking soft, pour in the stock, cover the pan and simmer for 25 minutes. Take the saucepan off the heat and liquidise the contents in your food processor. Unless you happen to have some sort of industrial machine this could take two loads, but don't return the liquidised mixture to your saucepan – rinse it and put it to one side. Smooth the curd cheese in the bottom of your rinsed saucepan and slowly stir in the liquidized soup until it's all incorporated and there are no lumps of curd cheese visible. Add the grated zest of the orange and stir. Return to the heat, simmer for a couple of minutes and serve.

Watercress Soup
(v)
Serves 4

If you're into colours, then this soup's a must – it's the most fantastic green and looks amazing in white soup bowls.

Ingredients
1 teaspoon olive oil
1 small onion, chopped
1 lb floury potatoes
1¾ pints vegetable stock
6 oz watercress
salt and pepper
¼ pint single cream

Method
In a large saucepan heat the olive oil and fry the onion in the olive oil for a couple of minutes until transparent. Peel and chop the potatoes into inch cubes. Add these to the pan, stir in and then pour over the stock. Add half the watercress, roughly chopped, and add a little salt and pepper. Bring to the boil and simmer for 10 minutes.

Pour the soup into a blender and process until it's smooth. Pour back two-thirds of the soup. Put the remaining watercress into the blender with the remaining soup and blend until the watercress is finely chopped. Then return the soup back to the pan and reheat, stirring slowly. Remove from the heat to add in the cream. Season to taste and serve.

Tip
I know it's obvious but colour really is important, so serve this soup with golden rolls.

Moules Marinières

Serves six slippery customers

I love mussels – they're fantastic and massively tasty, but they are a bit fiddly so this starter isn't the ideal one for those unexpected guests.

Ingredients
6 pints fresh mussels
1 oz butter
1 large onion, finely chopped
4 sprigs fresh parsley
2 sprigs fresh thyme
1 bay leaf
freshly ground black pepper
½ pint dry white wine
salt
chopped fresh parsley
fresh crusty bread to serve

Method

Scrape and clean each mussel with a strong knife, removing every trace of mud, seaweed and beard (fluffy cotton-like strands). Wash until the water runs clean.

Melt the butter in a large pan over a low heat. Add the onion to the pan and fry until soft but not coloured. Add the herbs, pepper, wine, salt and mussels. Cover with a tightly-fitting lid and cook quickly, shaking the pan constantly, until the mussels open. Any mussels which don't open are dead and should be discarded. This takes about 5 minutes. Lift the mussels out and discard the empty half of the shell. Keep hot in a covered dish. Boil the cooking liquid to reduce to about ½ pint (300 ml). Remove the herbs.

Beurre Manié:
1 oz creamed soft butter
½ oz flour

To make the Beurre Manié, blend the butter and flour together to a smooth paste. Drop into the simmering stock a teaspoonful at a time and whisk until the stock is smooth and has thickened. Taste and check seasoning and then pour over the mussels. Serve sprinkled with freshly chopped parsley and bread.

Note

Throw out any mussels which are badly cracked or that do not close firmly. The open ones are already dead and can't be eaten, there's nothing worse than being the cause of food poisoning!

Tortilla (v)

Serves 6

Fantastic, easy lunch menu for when your guests have decided not to leave from the night before and you find each other wandering about in the kitchen ravenously scouring the cupboards.

Ingredients

3 large, old and non-waxy potatoes
1 large Spanish onion
6 tablespoons olive oil
salt, to taste
5 medium-sized eggs

Method

Peel and dice the potatoes and finely chop the onion. Heat three tablespoons of oil in an omelette or non-stick frying pan. Add the potatoes and a pinch of salt and fry for a few minutes. Then add the onion, cover and cook over a moderate heat for about 15 minutes, stirring occasionally to avoid burning. Once the vegetables are cooked, drain off the excess oil.

In a separate bowl, beat the eggs and add the potato and onion mixture. Heat three tablespoons of oil and return to the pan. Cook on a low heat until the mixture is set and comes away from the sides of the pan. Scrape the edges of the tortilla with a fish slice to avoid it sticking to the pan. Put a plate over the frying pan and turn the tortilla onto it, then return it to the pan to cook on the other side. Serve when the base is cooked.

Tip

Tortillas have a nasty habit of burning and sticking and it can all become somewhat messy. The best thing to do is to gently rock the pan whilst the tortilla is cooking to try and stop the mixture sticking.

Cheesy Potato Skins
Serves 4

Great brunch recipe for when you're starving and unconcerned about your health.

Ingredients
3 medium-sized baking potatoes
vegetable oil
seasoned salt
4 oz grated Cheddar cheese
6 slices bacon, cooked and crumbled
large tub sour cream, to serve

Method
Scrub the potatoes thoroughly and rub skins with oil; bake at 400°F for 1 hour or until done. Allow the potatoes to cool until you can touch them. Cut them in half lengthways. Carefully scoop out the pulp, leaving ¼ to ⅛-inch shell. The pulp may be reserved for mashed potatoes or other uses (I can't think of any offhand). Cut the shells in half crosswise, and deep fry in hot oil (375°F) for 2 minutes or until lightly browned. Drain on paper towels. Place the skins on a baking sheet; sprinkle with salt, cheese and bacon. Then place them under the grill until the cheese melts. Serve with sour cream.

Garlic Mushrooms with Cream (v)
Serves 4 (as a starter) and 1 as a binge

A really easy starter, this always goes down well at dinner parties.

Ingredients
12 oz small button mushrooms
1½ oz butter
1 clove garlic, crushed
salt
freshly ground black pepper
¼ pint double cream
bread rolls, to serve

Method
Wash the mushrooms and trim the ends of the stalks. Melt the butter in a saucepan, add the garlic and mushrooms and cook for 5 minutes. Season well. Remove from the heat to stir in the cream and then simmer gently for a further 5 minutes or until the mushrooms are tender. Serve hot with bread rolls.

Tip
Use really perfect mushrooms if you can – it's worth it as shoddy ones will ruin the effect.

Baked Eggs and Cheese (v)

Serves 4

Simple and gorgeous.

Ingredients

margarine, for greasing the baking dish

1½ cups grated cheese (I like mozzarella or havarti)

¼ cup sliced onion

8 large eggs

⅔ cup semi-skimmed milk

Method

Preheat the oven to 350°F. Grease the bottom and the sides of an 8 x 8 x 2 inch baking dish with butter or margarine. Sprinkle half the cheese and all the onion over the bottom. Make eight slight impressions in the cheese/onion layer. Break the eggs, one by one, over each of their 'nests'. Pour the milk over the eggs and then sprinkle the remaining cheese over the top.

Bake the dish until the eggs are set – about 20–25 minutes (it may take up to 30 minutes). Serve hot.

Tip

Make sure that your eggs are fresh. To check, lower an egg into a bowl of water. If it lies on its side, it's quite fresh. However, if it stands on its end, it's less fresh. If it floats to the top, it's stale and you'll have to get some more.

Spinach and Carrot Timbale (v)

Serves 4

It's a bit of a faff but it's worth the effort to get the effect of the contrasting colours and flavours.

Ingredients
1 lb spinach
1 lb carrots
1 clove garlic, crushed
1 egg
juice of one orange
black pepper
sliced tomato

to garnish:
toasted sesame seeds

Method

Cook the spinach in boiling water for five minutes and drain. Slice the carrots into even-sized pieces and cook until tender (about 10 minutes). Liquidize the spinach, add the crushed garlic and egg with lots of black pepper, until a smooth puree is formed. Purée the carrots separately until they're smooth and soft. Season with black pepper and add the orange juice. Place a layer of carrot purée, then a layer of spinach purée into 4–6 small dishes. Pop in the microwave for just under a minute or cook in the oven at Gas Mark 6 for 15 minutes until the spinach purée is set. Garnish with the sliced tomato and sesame seeds.

Tip
If you want the dish to be more creamy, add some mayonnaise at the spinach puréeing stage.

Snacks and Picnics

Never underestimate the appeal of a snack – sandwiches can often be the most sumptuous meal of the day. There's a tremendous amount of mileage in a well-packed lunch-box with the added appeal of being able to dine *al fresco* at the location of your choice.

Tips for the perfect sandwich:
• Don't skimp – people notice that bit near the crust which has failed to make an acquaintance with the filling.
• Accessorize your sandwiches – that little bunch of chives could make all the difference.
• Invest in picnic paraphernalia – novelty cruets are a must.
• Have plenty 'on the side' gherkins, olives and mustard. This lessens the chance of your sandwich guest disliking your creation as they will virtually make it themselves and feel part of the whole experience.
• Cut off the crusts – it looks like you've made more of an effort.
• Always take a quantity of serviettes to mop up any indiscretions.
• Don't forget the perils of wasps.

As well as sandwiches, there are a multitude of other lunch-box delights to be partaken of, as described on the following pages.

Mexican Bean Salad (v)
Serves 3

Ingredients

1 x 14 oz tin kidney beans, drained

1 x 14 oz tin flageolet beans (great beans for that S&M theme), drained

7 chopped capers

2 cloves garlic, crushed

Juice of ½ lemon

½ cup olive oil

¼ cup white wine vinegar

2 baby gherkins, diced

For the health-conscious amongst us (it actually tastes pretty good as well).

Method
Whack the whole lot in a bowl and mix (make sure you've drained the beans first). Pop it in the fridge overnight and Bob's your uncle.

Home-made Mayonnaise (v)
This actually tastes much better than the stuff in jars.

Ingredients

2 egg yolks

1 level teaspoon Dijon mustard

1 level teaspoon salt

1 level teaspoon caster sugar

pepper

1 tablespoon white wine vinegar

½ pint sunflower oil

1 tablespoon lemon juice

Method
Put the yolks, mustard, salt, sugar and pepper in a bowl with the vinegar and mix well. Add the oil, drop by drop, beating well with a whisk the whole time until the mixture is smooth and thick, then beat in the lemon juice. This is particularly good wrist practice for lesbians.

Tip

I tend to cheat by using a food processor (my wrists are strong enough already).

Old-fashioned Game Pie

Serves as many as can stomach it.

This is not for the squeamish and especially inappropriate around vegetarians or fans of *Watership Down*.

Ingredients

Filling:

12 oz boneless rabbit, diced

12 oz belly of minced pork

12 oz pheasant, diced

6 oz streaky bacon, de-rinded and chopped

1 tablespoon chopped parsley

1 teaspoon chopped sage

1 teaspoon dried mixed herbs

2 tablespoons green peppercorns (if you've got them)

salt and pepper

4 tablespoons brandy (now you're talking)

Pastry:

1¼ lb plain flour

2 teaspoons salt

5 oz lard

¼ pint water

¼ pint milk

beaten egg, for glazing

Jellied Stock:

1 x 15oz tin consommé

1 teaspoon gelatine (now is hardly the time to worry about vegetarian gelatine)

Method

Put the meats, herbs, peppercorns and salt and pepper into a large bowl. Pour over the brandy and mix well. Cover and set aside.

Sift the flour and salt into a bowl. Put the lard, water and milk in a pan, bring just to the boil, pour into the bowl and mix well. Knead lightly. Cut off one third of the dough, cover with foil and keep on one side for the lid. Roll out the remaining dough on a floured surface to a 14 inch circle. Fold in quarters and use to line a deep 7 inch round, loose-bottomed cake tin, unfolding and shaping round the tin and leaving the dough overlapping the edge. Spoon in the meat mixture.

Roll out the remaining dough, dampen the edge and use to cover the pie, sealing the edges well. Trim off the excess pastry and pinch or flute the edges. Make a hole in the centre of the pie. Roll out the trimmings and use to decorate. Brush with the beaten egg and bake in a medium oven (Gas Mark 6) for 30 minutes. Lower the temperature to Gas Mark 4 and bake for 2 hours. If the top browns, cover with foil. Take the pie out of the oven and leave until completely cold.

Place the consommé in a pan, sprinkle over the gelatine and heat gently, stirring, until dissolved. Remove from the heat and leave until just on the point of setting, then pour through the hole of the pie.

Leave for 2 to 3 hours until set, then remove from the tin.

Cheese and Onion Bread Plait (v)

Makes two plaits

Ingredients

Dough:

1 lb strong plain flour

2 teaspoons salt

1 oz butter

2 teaspoons dried yeast

1 teaspoon caster sugar

½ pint warm milk

1 egg, beaten

Filling:

1 tablespoon oil

2 large onions, finely chopped

4 oz mature Cheddar cheese, grated

1 beaten egg, to glaze

Method

Sift the flour and salt into a bowl and rub in the butter until the mixture resembles breadcrumbs.

Combine the yeast, sugar and warm milk and leave in a warm place for about 10 minutes. Add the yeast mixture and one beaten egg to the flour and mix to a smooth dough. Turn onto a floured surface and knead for about 10 minutes until the dough is smooth and not sticky. Cover and leave to rise in a warm place for about 1¼ hours (or until it's doubled in size).

Meanwhile, heat the oil in a pan, add the onions and fry until golden. Leave to cool. When the onions are cool, retrieve the dough and knock into shape, add the onions and the grated cheese, distributing them fairly. Divide the dough in half, then divide each half into three. Now, it may have been a while since your last plait, but it all comes flooding back and in the end you'll have two plaits worthy of Rapunzel. Place them on a baking sheet, cover with a plastic bag and leave to rise in a warm place for 45 minutes. Brush with beaten egg and bake in a medium temperature oven for twenty minutes. Then brush with more beaten egg and return to the oven for another 20 minutes or until risen and golden brown.

Fairy Cakes

Donna's Mum's Boiled Fruit Cake

A novel cake idea – boiling's not something you'd usually expect from a cake recipe, but I can assure you that the result's absolutely gorgeous – really moist and fruity. Any fruit will do for this recipe – so it could be dates and walnuts instead of the traditional sultanas, etc. It's also possible to include a handful of nuts or cherries.

Ingredients
1 lb mixed fruit
4 oz butter or margarine
8 oz dark brown sugar
cup of tea
1 teaspoon mixed spice
8 oz self-raising flour
3 medium-sized eggs
cherries/nuts (optional)

Method
Grease a 7½-inch lined cake tin. Put the fruit, butter or margarine, sugar, tea and spice into a large saucepan. Bring to the boil and boil for 5 – 10 minutes. Take off the heat and allow to cool. When cool, add the flour, eggs and cherries or nuts if you're using them. Bake in a pre-heated oven (Gas Mark 3) for 1½ hours. When the mixture is cooked, allow it to stand for ½ hour, then remove from the tin to cool.

Tip
This cake is a lovely deep brown colour so there's no need to brown it in the oven – therefore, you can cover the tin in paper (tied at the top with string) to stop any potential burning while baking.

Peter Tatchell's Thai Banana and Nut Cake

The recipe for this sensuous, moist, sticky banana cake was originally given to me by a lover as a 'forget-me-not'. I've since passed it to others who I've subsequently loved as a memento of my affection.

Ingredients
3 oz butter
6 oz muscovado sugar
2 eggs (beaten)
6 oz self-raising wholemeal flour
1 ¼ teaspoons baking powder
½ teaspoon salt
½ teaspoon bicarbonate of soda
8 ripe bananas (mashed)
4 oz chopped hazelnuts/walnuts

Method

Melt the butter in a pan. Add the sugar to the melted butter, and pour into a large bowl or blender. Then add the eggs and mix well. Sift in the flour, baking powder, salt and bicarbonate of soda. Beat the mixture vigorously, until light and smooth. Fold in the bananas and chopped nuts. Pour the mixture into a greased cake tin (8 inch).

Cook the cake for 60 – 70 minutes at Gas Mark 4. Test the cake with a knife – the middle of the cake should be slightly sticky, when cooked.

Country Apple Crisp

Good, wholesome fodder, ideal for pretend family get-togethers on autumn evenings.

Ingredients

1 large orange

7 medium-sized golden delicious apples peeled, cored, and cut into 1-inch slices

½ cup dried cherries or raisins

1 teaspoon ground cinnamon

½ teaspoon salt

¼ teaspoon ground nutmeg

⅓ cup packed light brown sugar

2 tablespoons wholemeal flour

Topping

½ cup porridge oats, uncooked

⅓ cup wholemeal flour

¼ cup packed light brown sugar

3 tablespoons margarine or butter

Method

Preheat oven to 425°F. Grate ½ teaspoon of peel from the orange; squeeze enough juice for ⅓ cup. In a 2-quart glass or ceramic baking dish, toss orange peel, orange juice, apple slices, cherries, cinnamon, salt, nutmeg, ⅓ cup packed light brown sugar and 2 tablespoons flour.

In a small bowl, mix the oats, flour and sugar for the topping. With a pastry blender or two knives used scissor-fashion, cut in the margarine or butter until the mixture resembles coarse crumbs. Sprinkle over the apple mixture.

Bake the Apple Crisp for 30 to 35 minutes until the apples are tender and the topping is lightly browned. Cover with foil, if necessary, to prevent overbrowning. Leave to cool and crisp slightly on wire rack. Serve warm or, cool. Crisp completely on the Apple Rack to serve later. Reheat, if desired.

Kathy Danger's Ravini

We call this 'ravine' in my family, just for fun, I'm an American Cypriot and this is a Greek cake. My sister gave me the recipe and it's really easy to make. She used to bake it when I was a kid.

Ingredients

Cake:
1 cup sugar
1 cup farina
1 cup flour
5 eggs
½ lb butter, melted
teaspoon vanilla or almond essence
a squeeze of lemon
1 teaspoon baking powder

Syrup:
3 cups water
1 cup sugar
1 squeeze lemon
½ teaspoon vanilla or almond essence
sugar almonds, to decorate

Method

Cake
Butter and flour a 9-inch square baking tin. Mix all the cake ingredients together by hand and pour into the tin. Bake in a pre-heated oven at 350°F for 40–45 minutes. Check the centre with a toothpick to see if it's cooked through.

Syrup
Cook all the ingredients on a low heat for ½ to ¾ hour and pour over the cooked cake.

Cut the cake into squares and decorate with coated sugar almonds.

Carrot Cake

The great thing about carrot cake is that you pretend to be healthy whilst noshing loads of gooey stodge – just the mention of the word 'carrot' summons up the unreal concept of 'health'.

Ingredients

8 oz self-raising flour
2 level teaspoons baking powder
5 oz light soft brown sugar
2 oz walnuts, chopped
4 oz carrots, washed, trimmed and grated (it's food processor time!)
2 ripe bananas, mashed
2 eggs
¼ pint corn oil

Topping:
3 oz soft butter or margarine
3 oz rich cream cheese
6 oz icing sugar, sieved
½ teaspoon vanilla essence

Method

Heat the oven to Gas Mark 4. Grease and line an 8-inch round cake tin. Sift together the flour and baking powder into a large bowl and stir in the sugar. Add the nuts, carrots and bananas and mix lightly. Make a well in the centre and add the eggs and oil. Beat well until thoroughly blended.

Turn the tin and bake in the oven for about 1¼ hours until golden brown. When cooked, the cake will have shrunk slightly from the sides of the tin and a warm skewer pierced in the centre of it will come out clean. Turn out the cake and remove the paper and then leave to cool on a wire rack.

Topping:

Place all the ingredients together in a bowl and beat well until blended and smooth. Spread over the cool cake and rough up with a fork. Harden slightly by cooling before serving.

Tip

To line a tin, take a piece of greaseproof paper. Place your cake tin on it and draw round the bottom. Cut the shape out with scissors and grease it for the bottom. Then measure the depth with a pencil or piece of string and cut a strip to fit.

D a t e   O a t m e a l
C o o k i e s
Makes 2 dozen

For those health freaks who don't
want to cut out cakes, but do want
to fill themselves with fibre.

Ingredients
1 cup pitted dates
1 cup fresh orange juice
3 cups rolled oats
1 cup flour
½ teaspoon baking soda
pinches of cinnamon,
nutmeg, cloves and ginger
pinch salt
½ cup oil
margarine, for greasing

M e t h o d
Rinse and drain the dates and put
them in a saucepan. Pour the orange
juice over the dates, cover and bring
to a simmer. Combine the oats and
other dry ingredients in a bowl.

When the dates are soft, pour them
into a blender. Add the oil and
purée until smooth. Pour this mixture over the oats and mix until well
coated.

Shape into small biscuits and place
on greased baking tray. Bake at
350°F for 12–15 minutes.

Glyn's Lemon Cake

Renowned throughout Edinburgh, the infamous Lemon Cake was often requested (as a substitute donation for a bottle of wine) at dinner parties during my undergraduate years. A sweet and sticky treat happily accepted at all times of the day: elevenses, with afternoon gossip, or soaking up dinner party booze. One of my best friends (much enamoured of this simple recipe – which until now has remained a secret) suggested that, in the far and distant future, money will have been replaced as the valid currency by sections of Lemon Cake.

Ingredients
6 oz self-raising flour
6 oz sugar (caster)
4 oz margarine
2 medium-sized eggs
1 heaped teaspoon baking powder
grated rind of 1 lemon

Icing
4 oz caster sugar
juice of 1 lemon

Method

Beat all the cake ingredients together in a bowl until the consistency is smooth. Line a cake tin with foil. Pour in the mixture. Bake at 180°C / Gas Mark 4 for 45–50 minutes until springy to touch.

Whilst the cake is cooking, make the icing. In a cup, stir the caster sugar into the juice of the lemon. Remove the cake from the oven and – while it's still hot – pour the sugar/lemon syrup over the top evenly. This should soak into the cake, leaving a thin, sugary crust on top.

Tip

If you want an extra-rich-spoil-yourself dish, serve it with double cream – but it's just perfect on it's own, thank you.

Chocolate Cake

This basic cake's a winner and you can vary it with different toppings or add nuts to the mixture.

Ingredients

Cake:
1 oz cocoa
2 tablespoons hot water
4 oz soft margarine
4 oz caster sugar
2 large eggs
4 oz self-raising flour
1 level teaspoon baking powder

Filling:
¼ pint whipping cream, whipped

Icing:
1½ oz soft margarine
1 oz cocoa, sieved
2 tablespoons milk
4 oz icing sugar, sieved

Method

Heat the oven to Gas Mark 4. Grease two 7-inch round sandwich tins and line them with greaseproof paper.

Blend the cocoa with the hot water in a large bowl and leave to cool. Add the remaining cake ingredients to the bowl and beat with a wooden spoon for 2 to 3 minutes until thoroughly blended. Turn into the tins and then bake in the oven for 25 to 30 minutes. When cooked, the cake will spring back when lightly pressed with a finger. Turn out, remove the paper and leave to cool on a wire rack. Sandwich the cakes together with the whipped cream.

For the icing: melt the margarine in a small saucepan, stir in the cocoa and cook over a gentle heat for one minute. Remove from the heat and add the milk and icing sugar. Beat well to mix and then leave to cool, stirring occasionally, until the icing has thickened to a spreading consistency. Spread over the top of the cake and swirl attractively with a round-bladed knife. Leave to set.

T i p
The topping's really up to you – you could just as easily use butter icing with cocoa powder in it.

Simon's Grandma's Hot Apple Pie

Never fails to please, there's nothing like home-grown Americana.

Ingredients

Pastry:
2 cups flour
½ teaspoon salt
6 tablespoons vegetable shortening
2 tablespoons cold butter
4 or 5 tablespoons ice-cold water

Filling:
4 cups tart (or cooking) apples
4 tablespoons flour
1¼ cups sugar
1 teaspoon cinnamon
¼ teaspoon nutmeg
⅛ teaspoon salt
4 tablespoons butter

Mix the flour and salt in a bowl. Add the shortening and butter. With a pastry blender or fork, cut the butter and shortening into the flour until it's crumbly. Gradually add cold water one tablespoon at a time until the dough holds together. Knead the dough very lightly and form into two balls. Wrap in cellophane and refrigerate for at least one hour.

On a floured board, roll out one ball of pastry and fit into the bottom of a 9-inch cake tin. Trim the edges with a sharp knife. Peel the apples, core and cut them into eighths. They should not be sliced too thinly. Combine the flour, sugar, spices and salt. Spread about half of this mixture over the unbaked crust bottom. Add the apples, sprinkling the remaining dry mixture over them. Dot with butter. Roll out the remaining pastry and cover the apples, sealing the edges carefully.

Cut a few slits in the top crust to allow steam to escape. Remove any excess pastry with the sharp knife. Crimp the edges with your thumbs to seal the pie. Bake in a preheated 425°F oven for 40 to 50 minutes, or until golden.

Fishy Dishes

Salmon with Pistou and a Tomato Sauce

Serves 4 (If you feel like splashing out.)

Ingredients
36 basil leaves
6 cloves of garlic,
inner green parts removed
6 tablespoons olive oil
salt, pepper and cayenne
2 white new-season onions
4 very ripe tomatoes
water
2 salmon steaks
½ oz unsalted butter
sprig of fresh thyme

Method

Pistou: put the basil, peeled garlic, olive oil and some salt and pepper into a liquidizer or food processor. Work the machine until you have a fairly thick purée.

Sauce: slice the onions, cut the tomatoes into quarters and put them with the onions into a saucepan on the stove. Add a scant ¼ pint of water, cook until the tomatoes have softened to a pulp, sieve and set it aside.

Skin the salmon and bone it. Cut each piece in two horizontally. Arrange the fish in an oven dish smeared with olive oil. (The oven dish needs to be made of a thin metal that conducts heat quickly.) Season with salt, pepper and cayenne, and put a dab of butter on to each piece of fish.

Finishing: Pre-heat the oven to 400°F. Leave the salmon in the oven for two minutes, then take it out again. It will continue to cook while you finish the sauces. Reheat the tomato sauce. Season it with salt, pepper, cayenne and fresh thyme. Bring it briefly to the boil. The pistou can be eaten hot or cold. To heat it, whisk it while it warms up over a low heat.

Serving: Serve each piece of salmon with a little tomato sauce underneath it. Coat with the pistou.

Linda Bellos's
Chilli Salmon
Serves 4

I like inventing dishes, particularly when we're inviting friends round. My partner and I have been together for five years and, regrettably, my desire to invent new dishes for her has waned, however when we first became lovers I was much more creative.

This dish consists of filleted salmon (as opposed to steaks). You can use farmed but it's best to go for fresh fish when they're in season. It's quite expensive so it's best reserved for special guests.

Ingredients
1 lb fresh salmon
bunch of spring onions
¼ lb mushrooms, sliced (or quartered, if small)
2 teaspoons capers
2 red chilli peppers
tablespoon crème fraîche

Method
Wash and trim the salmon. Take the scales off but leave the skins on. Cut the fillets into 2-inch-wide slices. Chop the spring onions and the mushrooms and capers, and put them in the base of a flattish casserole dish. Place the salmon on top and then place the chopped chilli on top of the salmon. Cover lightly with the crème fraîche. Cook for 35–40 minutes in a medium oven. Serve with new potatoes and broccoli or beans and a salad.

Tip
If you don't like your food to be too hot, then take the seeds out of the chillies. Always remember to wash your hands after cutting chillies – especially before removing contact lenses!

Crab Cakes
Serves 4

Ingredients

3 tablespoons
diced red peppers

3 tablespoons diced shallots

1 tablespoon
cooking sherry

1 egg

¼ cup cream

3 tablespoons lemon juice

dash Tabasco

pinch celery salt

½ teaspoon paprika

pinch ground white pepper

pinch salt

3 tablespoons
chopped parsley

1 lb Dungeness crab
meat (break up larger pieces)

½ cup fine breadcrumbs

butter, for sautéing

Method

In a bowl mix the red peppers and
shallots together. Then mix together
all the other ingredients, except the
crab and breadcrumbs, thoroughly.
Add the crab and mix. Form into
patties (about 2 oz (56 g) each). Pat
the breadcrumbs onto crab cakes.
Store between wax paper sheets until
ready to cook. Pan-sauté in melted
butter until brown on both sides.

Great served with a light pepper
salad and French dressing.

Grilled Fillets of Dace or Trout with Tarragon
Serves 4

Ingredients

4 tablespoons whipping cream, whipped

2 egg yolks

1¾ oz unsalted butter

4 fillets of dace or trout (each weighing 80–90 g)

salt and pepper

2 teaspoons chopped tarragon leaves

½ lemon

about ½ pint dry white wine

¼ pint double cream

Note: as an alternative to dace, you could use freshwater trout or pike, but the trout must have white, rather than pink flesh.

Method

Pre-heat the oven to 530°F. Set aside 3 tablespoons of the whipped cream; beat the egg yolks with the remainder. Butter an oven dish with ¾ oz of the butter. Arrange the fillets on the top and season them. Add the white wine.

Slide the dish containing the fish into the pre-heated oven. Leave it for 1½ – 2 minutes or longer, depending on the thickness of the fish (the oven dish needs to be made of a thin metal that conducts heat quickly). Take it out and remove the skins from the fish. Put the fish into a shallow dish and keep it hot.

Pour the liquid that remains in the cooking dish into a saucepan. Add the tarragon and reduce the liquid by about two-thirds. Whisk in 1 oz of cold, diced butter and the remaining whipped cream. Let the sauce reduce for a moment, then pour it, still whisking, onto the egg-yolk-and-cream mixture.

Put the sauce back into a saucepan over a very gentle heat and let it thicken, whisking all the time, until it shows signs of boiling. Remove from the stove, and season with salt, pepper and a little lemon juice. Carefully incorporate the whipped cream and the dry white wine.

Pre-heat the grill. Ladle the sauce over the fish, place it under the grill and leave it until the sauce turns golden. This will only take about 1 minute, so watch carefully. Serve at once.

Garlic-roasted Whole Dungeness Crab
Serves 1

Now this recipe is a treat, if you want to spoil yourself and aren't particularly concerned about the welfare of crabs in general or about splashing out on what, quite frankly, is something of a delicacy.

Ingredients
1 Dungeness crab
4 cups extra virgin olive oil
½ cup chopped fresh garlic
3 tablespoons salt
1 tablespoon freshly ground white pepper
1 tablespoon crushed red pepper
2 tablespoons chopped fresh thyme
2 tablespoons chopped fresh tarragon
2 tablespoons chopped parsley
1 cup fresh lemon juice

Method
Remove and clean the top shell of the crab. Prepare a marinade by combining all the other ingredients. Leave the crab in the marinade for 4 hours. Heat the oven to 450°F. Place the crab in the oven dish with ½ cup of the marinade. Roast the crab in the oven for about 15–20 minutes.

Put on your favourite song and pour yourself a glass of your favourite wine – pure self-indulgence.

Swiss Tuna Grill
Serves 6

Ingredients

1 x 6½ oz can tuna, drained and flaked

½ cup (about 2 oz) shredded Swiss cheese

½ cup finely chopped celery

2 tablespoons finely chopped onion

¼ cup mayonnaise

¼ cup sour cream

dash of pepper

12 slices rye bread

butter or margarine, softened

Method

Combine tuna, cheese, celery, onion, mayonnaise, sour cream and pepper, stirring well. Spread the mixture on 6 slices of bread and top with the remaining bread slices. Spread butter on the outer sides of bread and grill over medium heat in a large frying pan until browned, turning once.

Easy Peasy!

Seafood Stirfry
Serves two hungry dykes

Amazingly simple – and only takes 5 minutes to cook from start.

Ingredients

cooking oil

1 onion (chopped)

handful mangetout

handful baby sweetcorn

small amount thinly sliced white cabbage (to add more crunch)

½ lb mixed seafood: mussels, cockles (squid is my favourite)

2 tablespoons soy sauce

½ bottle oyster sauce and a handful of crab sticks (chopped)

Method

In a wok or shallow frying pan, heat the oil until fairly hot, but not smoking. Stir-fry the onion, mangetout, sweetcorn and cabbage for 2 minutes, then add the seafood and soy sauce. Carry on frying for another 2 minutes and then, at the end, add ½ bottle oyster sauce and crab sticks and fry for 2 minutes more. (The reason for adding the crab sticks at the end is that they go soggy very quickly otherwise.)

Serve immediately the sauce has heated through... DELICIOUS!
You can serve with rice or noodles (although we have ours with pitta bread and we're happy).

No Exactamente Paella (Not Exactly Paella)

Serves 4

Ingredients

½ lb medium prawns in the shell

water

1½ tablespoons salt

bay leaf

1 clove garlic, crushed

either ½ cup milk and ¼ teaspoon Spanish saffron *or* 1 medium tomato, chopped

½ – 1 lb of nice sausages, your favourite kind (I love Italian Chorizo sausages)

olive oil

1½ cups long grain rice

white wine

6–10 clams

Note:
Use a large frying pan or sauteuse, with a good cover.

Method

Peel the prawns. Put the shells into a small saucepan and cover well with water. Add the salt, bay leaf and garlic and bring to a boil. Reduce to simmering and cover.

Use either saffron or tomato to add colour. If you use saffron, heat the milk to a bit less than boiling and add the saffron to it. If you use tomato, add it to the broth now.

Pierce the sausages and fry them gently in some olive oil in the frying pan for 10 minutes. Then add ½ cup of wine, bring to a boil, reduce to a low simmer, and cover.

Have a glass of wine while the sausages steam and the broth is simmering away.

When the sausages have steamed for 15 minutes or so, take them out of the pan and set them aside. If there is still water in the pan, cook it off. Then if there is a lot of grease in the pan, pour it off but DON'T clean the pan! Slice the sausages into ½-inch slices, unless they are already quite small in size.

> *Tip*
> **The thing that's so inauthentic about this is that it's made on top of the stove, not baked. Also, I don't use chicken, though it would be easy to add this.**

Strain the broth into a measuring cup. You want 2½ cups if you're using saffron and milk, 3 cups otherwise. If you have less than that, add water and if you have more, cook it down some more with the cover off.

When your broth is ready, put a few tablespoons of olive oil in the frying pan and heat over high heat. Add the rice and stir continuously until the grains turn from translucent to a bright, opaque white. Immediately add the broth (careful, it may spatter as it hits the hot pan). Add the milk and saffron, if used. Stir once, and as soon as the broth boils again, reduce heat to a low simmer and cover.

Have another glass of wine. After the rice has simmered for about 10 minutes, add the sausages and cover again. After another 10 minutes, add the clams.

After 10 minutes, peek and see if the clams have opened. If they haven't, give them a little more time.

When the clams have opened, add the prawns. Cover and cook for maybe 2 minutes. As soon as the prawns have definitely turned pink, put the pan on the table and call in the troops. By the time they sit down the prawns will be perfect.

Main Meals

Michelangelo Signorile's Cavatelle David (v)

(Serves two muscle queens,
four of everything else)

This recipe has been in my family forever but it never had a name, so I decided I'd name it after my boyfriend because I feed it to him every week. It's a Southern Italian peasant meal – my family has all these cheap fast meals that make you full. It's perfect for freezing New York winter days because it's low fat/high protein, light and delicious.

Ingredients

½ lb broccoli

½ lb carrots (you can use up to 1½ lb)

1lb Cavatelle pasta (you can substitute shells)

2 tablespoons olive oil

2 tablespoons chopped onions

3 cloves garlic, crushed

2 cups breadcrumbs

1 tablespoon chopped basil

½ teaspoon black pepper

couple pinches salt

teaspoon dried rosemary (optional)

2 tablespoons grated Parmesan cheese

Method

Chop the vegetables into chunks (slice the carrots into four and slice the stems of the broccoli in two and cut off the branches). Steam the vegetables for 20 minutes or boil. Simultaneously boil the pasta in a pan of water until tender. In a saucepan, heat the olive oil on a low flame. Add the chopped onions and the garlic, cook until brown. Take two cups of breadcrumbs, basil, salt, pepper and rosemary (optional) and add to the saucepan with the onions and garlic. Cook on a low to medium flame until the breadcrumbs are toasted (keep stirring so they're all evenly cooked). All three pans should be ready at the same time. Drain the pasta, add the vegetables, grated Parmesan and breadcrumb mix, and stir.

Tip

The key to this dish is ensuring that all the breadcrumbs are equally well browned. I like to drink Chardonnay with it, my boyfriend likes to drink Merlot with it – it goes with either.

Adam's Useful Networking Meal
Serves 2

Pear and Cheese Starter

A simple but sophisticated starter – easy to make, leaving plenty of time to casually discuss important issues.

Ingredients

6 conference pears (pealed, cored and halved)

6 oz Roquefort cheese

Method

Lay out the pears on an ovenproof dish. On each pear half, place a slab of Roquefort cheese (in the crater where the core was). Grill for 10 minutes until the cheese has melted. Serve with a crisp white wine (possibly a South African Sauvignon Blanc) – to add a touch of political savvy.

Tip
You can cheat with a tin of pears – but don't forget to hide the tin before the guest arrives.

Chicken and Lemon

A cheap, but substantial and mouth-watering meal for someone you have no intention of getting it on with later. Ideal for knobbling committee meetings by leaving your guest with an overwhelming sense of debt to you.

Ingredients

4 – 6 oz mushrooms (depending on how much you like them)

1 clove garlic

2 oz seasoned flour

2 boneless chicken breasts

2 tablespoons olive oil

teaspoon lemon juice (or more to taste)

teaspoon fresh parsley, chopped

Method

Slice the mushrooms & crush the garlic. Place the seasoned flour in a bowl and turn the chicken breasts in it until they're completely sealed. Heat the oil in a frying pan on a low heat. Fry the chicken and the garlic until the chicken is white on the outside and the garlic is browning. Add the mushrooms. Cook for 10 minutes or until the chicken is cooked through. Remove the chicken and mushrooms and place in a warmed bowl. Turn up the heat, add the lemon juice and parley – jussh at full pelt for 2 – 3 minutes. Swiftly pour the hot sauce over the chicken. Serve with new potatoes, a bundle of fresh green vegetables and a fine Sancerre ('92).

Brian's Creamy Fishy Spinach
Serves 4

Ingredients
extra virgin olive oil

1 lb nice pasta – probably butterflies (Farfalle)

1 lb mushrooms

glass of white wine

large pot extra thick double cream

salt and pepper

big pack of spinach

fresh basil

2 slices smoked salmon

mature Cheddar cheese, grated

I was living in a shared house in London's Stoke Newington – I was the cleaner and there was a really big house meeting about the cleaning and I didn't want to go, so I stayed downstairs and cooked the others a meal.

Method
Boil some water in a pan, then put on the pasta. Put some virgin olive oil in a big wok and fry the mushrooms for about 5 minutes until they go soft. Pour in the glass of wine and reduce it by half, then put the double cream in and simmer it for about 10 minutes until it goes nice and thick. Then season with salt and pepper.

Rip up the spinach and the basil (make sure you've washed the spinach really well because it always tends to have mud in it). Slice the salmon and put the spinach, basil and salmon in the wok and toss until they're coated, but still crunchy (2 minutes). Then mix in the pasta and sprinkle the grated cheese on the top.

Serve with Tomato & Mozzarella Salad.

Tomato and Mozarella Salad with Brian's Basily Dressing

Dressing
fresh basil
2 fl oz virgin olive oil
1 fl oz white wine vinegar
2 cloves garlic, crushed
salt and pepper

Salad
4 beef tomatoes
packet mozzarella (Italian) cheese
2 avocados

Method
Rip up the basil leaves (about 5 of them) and mix the dressing together in a used glass jar. Shake thoroughly. Leave in the fridge for several hours.

Slice the salad ingredients and arrange artistically.

Caponata (v)
Serves 2 – 3

This is the best version of this recipe I've ever tasted. An excellent first course served on lettuce-lined plates. It may also be used as a stuffing for tomatoes to accompany meat dishes.

Ingredients
olive oil
1 medium aubergine, unpeeled, finely chopped
1 large onion, coarsely chopped
½ cup coarsely chopped mushrooms
1 chopped green pepper
2 cloves garlic, crushed
½ cup chopped stuffed green olives
¼ cup chopped black olives
¼ cup drained capers
3 tablespoons pine nuts
small tin tomato purée
⅓ cup water
2 tablespoons red wine vinegar
2 teaspoons sugar
1½ teaspoons salt
½ teaspoon pepper
½ teaspoon dried oregano

Method

I use just enough oil to keep the vegetables from sticking to the pan. Because they have such a high water content, they quickly provide moisture in the pan. In a large enamel saucepan, combine the aubergine, onion, mushrooms, green pepper, garlic and oil. Simmer with the pan covered for 10 minutes. Add all the remaining ingredients; mix well and simmer with the pan covered for a further 25 minutes, stirring occasionally. The aubergine should be cooked but not overly soft. Refrigerate overnight (it may be frozen).

Claire's Vegetarian Cannelloni (v)
Serves 6

When my partner and I had our relationship blessed, I asked some friends to make something vegetarian and they came along with this.

Ingredients

Maria Esposito's Tomato Sauce

2 standard size tubs of ricotta cheese

½ lb spinach, blanched and chopped

juice of ½ lemon

green pepper, chopped

14 oz can black olives, roughly chopped

3 tablespoons freshly grated Parmesan cheese

½ cup grated Cheddar cheese

1 box cannelloni

Method

Make a standard tomato sauce (see Maria Esposito's Tomato Sauce page 94.) with 3 tins of tomatoes. Mix together the ricotta, spinach, lemon juice, green pepper, black olives and Parmesan. Gently stuff the cannelloni with a knife (this is one of the most restful activities in the world) and, in a large ovenproof dish, cover the base with tomato sauce and place the cannelloni side by side with the rest of the tomato sauce over the top. Then cover that with a mixture of cheddar and fresh Parmesan. Cook in a medium oven for 40 minutes.

Serve with a fresh salad with whatever wine you fancy. It's just as good from frozen.

Tips
If your friends really do arrive totally unannounced, you can mix pesto in the tomato sauce to bulk it up. If you're not exactly a vegetarian, you can add in a can of tuna to the cannelloni stuffing.

Polenta à la Juno
(v)
Serves 4

Ingredients
1lb polenta
olive oil
1 medium onion (sliced)
1 green pepper
1 red pepper
1 small aubergine
3–4 courgettes
2 beef tomatoes
oregano
sour cream (small pot)
wild or regular rice, French dressing and roasted peanuts, to serve

This is a gorgeous Italian rustic recipe – just the sort of thing for eating out on the farm. It's served traditionally with pigeon or rabbit. You can either buy the maize flour and make the polenta from scratch. Or just go to an Italian deli and it costs less than a pound for 1lb, which should easily serve four people. It's unbelievably tasty and you just won't want your dinner to end.

Method
Slice the polenta into four and deep-fry it in the olive oil. When it's brown and golden, take it out. Meanwhile slice the onion, roughly chop the peppers, aubergine, courgettes and beef tomatoes. Fry them in olive oil till they're softening but not too soft, then season with oregano. Serve the vegetable mixture on the polenta and pour over the sour cream.

This dish is ideally served with wild rice or regular rice: dress the rice with a basic French dressing to give it some piquancy and add a handful of roasted peanuts.

Rick Richardson's Shrimp Pasta with Sun-Dried Tomatoes
Serves 4

Ingredients
1 lb pasta (spaghettini works best)

3 tablespoons of olive oil

3 tablespoons of butter

4 – 6 cloves of garlic, minced (or more if your date is eating with you!)

1 x 8oz bottle of clam juice

1 lb raw shrimp

juice of 2 lemons

1 cup sun-dried tomatoes, soaked in water and chopped

1 bunch parsley, finely chopped

salt and pepper

This is a winner for entertaining guests because:
a) they'll think you've transformed into the Lord of the Kitchen, and
b) most of the work can be done hours before, taking only about 10 minutes away from your company for final preparation.

Method
Cook the pasta until firm, drain and toss in a little olive oil so it doesn't stick together. Set aside. Have all the other ingredients ready to go for when it's ... Showtime: then heat the butter and olive oil and sauté the garlic for about three minutes in a large skillet or wok. Toss in the shrimp and cook until pink throughout. Throw in the pasta, clam juice, lemon juice, tomatoes, parsley, and stir until heated throughly. Add salt and pepper to taste, and serve with a light salad, some wonderful bread, and call it dinner!

If this doesn't get ya laid, at least it will keep the Vampire Lestat at bay ...

Juno's Bone Idle Peanut Chicken
Serves 4

This is incredibly easy to make and tastes delicious, both hot and cold.

Ingredients
4 boned, skinned, chicken fillets
seasoned flour
olive oil
1 teaspoon lemon juice
14 oz can chopped tomatoes
2 cloves garlic (crushed)
1 onion (chopped)
1 green pepper (chopped)
(anything else you fancy to make the sauce – could be mushrooms, courgettes, what ever you happen to have around)
2 – 3 tablespoons crunchy peanut butter
1 tablespoon curry sauce
(from the jars that you buy in supermarkets and stain the labels)

To serve:
4 baking potatoes
sour cream
chives

Method
Turn the chicken fillets in the seasoned flour and brown them in some olive oil in a large casserole dish (sprinkle with the lemon juice). When they're browned put them to one side and put the tomatoes, garlic, onion and other vegetables into the casserole and cook for about 25 minutes until they're soft. Return the chicken to the casserole with the peanut butter and the curry sauce, then stir and simmer for between 5 – 10 minutes.

Serve with baked potatoes filled with sour cream and chives

Simon's Alfredo Pasta (v)

Serves 4

It always impresses people when I use words like 'Alfredo' instead of cream, so despite the fact that this sauce is fantastically simple, it never ceases to be appreciated.

Ingredients
8 oz pasta (Farfalle is good)
2oz butter
1 cup Parmesan cheese
1 pint whipping cream
nutmeg, to serve

Method

Cook the pasta in a saucepan and drain thoroughly.

Melt the butter in another pan and slowly add cheese, cream and cooked pasta. You need to add the cheese slowly so it doesn't form clumps. I have modified this recipe by taking out all the butter and using whipping cream and milk instead of all whipping cream. It doesn't taste as good but it's not nearly as bad for you. Sprinkle with nutmeg to serve.

A most unlikely bunch of
ingredients

3 lb chuck roast, or sirloin,
rolled, or whatever steak.

cooking oil

2 cups water

1 can beer

1 can tomato sauce

½ cup or so chopped onion

¼ cup sugar

2 tablespoons vinegar

2 teaspoons salt

1½ teaspoons cinnamon

3 bay leaves

½ teaspoon ground pepper

¾ teaspoon ground ginger

cornstarch and water

Jim and David's Illinois Supper
Serves Jim and David

Jim Donovan and David Moore
have been together for 20+ years.
Jim's originally from Lexington KY
and David's from Nashville. They
are both Church organists – in fact,
that is how they met: at a meeting
of the American Guild of Organists.
They have a small farm in Plainville
IL, about 15 miles from Quincy and
Hannibal MO. They raise most of
their own vegetables, and Jim does a
lot of canning and preserving. Dave
is an administrator at Quincy
University. They have three German
shepherd dogs (Alsatians) and one
13-year-old cat who acts as if he
were three. The dogs keep David on
the run, but he incites them! Jim's a
piano and pipe organ service techni-
cian, so they are both busy.

Bavarian Pot Roast

Method

In a Dutch oven, brown the roast in
the oil; combine water, beer, tomato
sauce, onion, sugar, vinegar, salt,
cinnamon, bay leaves, pepper and
ginger. Pour over meat and bring to
a boil. Reduce heat; cover and simmer until meat is tender, for 2½ to 3
hours. Remove meat; discard bay
leaves. Thicken sauce if desired with
cornstarch and water.

Baked Sweet & Sour Brussels Sprouts (v)

(Sounds repulsive, but is really delicious)

Ingredients

1 packet (10 oz) frozen Brussels sprouts

3 tablespoons oil

¼ cup vinegar

2 tablespoons sugar

½ teaspoon salt

¼ teaspoon pepper

Parmesan cheese

shredded Swiss cheese

Arrange the sprouts in shallow baking dish. Combine the oil, vinegar, sugar, salt and pepper; pour over sprouts. Cover with a good layer of Parmesan cheese and then a good layer of shredded Swiss cheese. Cover and marinate for several hours, or overnight. Bake about 45 minutes at 375°F.

Beer Cheese (HOT!) (v)

Ingredients

1 lb sharp longhorn cheese, grated

1 teaspoon red pepper

1 teaspoon chilli powder

1 teaspoon red hot sauce

2 minced garlic cloves

1 small onion (grind with cheese)

1 can stale beer

Method

Mix all the ingredients and chill.

Cheese and Lentil Gratin (v)

Serves 4

Good for a '70s dyke reunion (until you realize they're all post vegetarian and *only* eat meat these days).

Ingredients
1 tablespoon oil
1 onion, chopped
1 carrot, chopped
1 celery stick, chopped
6 oz red lentils
1 clove garlic, crushed
¼ pt water or stock
4 oz grated Cheddar cheese
2 tablespoons chopped parsley (preferably flat Italian)
1 medium egg, beaten
salt and pepper
2 tablespoons wholemeal breadcrumbs
2 teaspoons sesame seeds

Method

Heat the oil in a pan, add the onion and fry till soft. Add carrot, celery, lentils, garlic and water (or stock) and cover. Bring to the boil, then simmer for 20 minutes or until all water is absorbed. Add 3 oz of the cheese, the parsley and the egg to the lentil mixture and stir thoroughly. Season well and spoon into a 1½ pint shallow ovenproof dish and smooth the top.

Mix the breadcrumbs with sesame seeds and the remaining cheese and sprinkle over the top. Bake in preheated oven at 180°C/350°F/Gas Mark 4 for 45 minutes until topping is golden brown and crisp. Serve hot or cold with a crisp green salad.

Ingredients
1 lb tomatoes
half a cucumber, peeled
6 oz feta cheese
3 tablespoons olive oil
salt and pepper
10 black olives, halved
1 tablespoon white wine vinegar
2 tablespoons chopped marjoram

Greek Salad (v)

Serves 4

Method

Quarter the tomatoes, slice the cucumber and dice the cheese. Place them in a bowl with the rest of the ingredients and stir well.

Simple, but super.

Ingredients

Vegetables:

1 large onion, coarsely chopped

24 fl oz vegetable stock

3 celery stalks, sliced into ½ inch pieces

3 carrots, peeled and coarsely chopped

4 cloves garlic, crushed

3 small turnips, peeled and coarsley chopped

1 red pepper, coarsely chopped

1 green pepper, coarsely chopped

1 yellow pepper, coarsely chopped

1 head fennel (just the inner leaves, sliced into ½ inch pieces)

¼ teaspoon allspice

1 lb courgettes, sliced into ½ inch pieces

½ cup chopped parsley (I prefer the flat stuff)

1 large (15 oz) tin chickpeas, drained

1½ teaspoons ground coriander

1 teaspoon paprika

6 tablespoons fresh lemon juice

1 teaspoon turmeric

¼ teaspoon ground ginger

¼ teaspoon ground cayenne pepper

Couscous:

¾ lb couscous and 24 fl oz boiling vegetable stock

Vegetarian Couscous (v)
Serves 4

Although it's extremely impressive to not only own a 'couscousière' but know how to both pronounce and use it, the truth is that you don't need one to cook great couscous. This is a particular favourite with my veggie dyke friends.

Method
Fry the onion until it's transparent, stir in 10 fl oz of the stock and let it bubble up. Stir in the celery, carrots, garlic, turnips, peppers, fennel and allspice. Turn the heat down and simmer, stirring frequently until the mixture is thick and the vegetables are frying in their own juices. Stir in the remaining ingredients and stock, cover and simmer for 20 minutes.

In a bowl combine the couscous with boiling stock and let infuse for 10 – 15 minutes until the liquid is absorbed and the grains are tender; fluff it up with a fork. Serve the couscous in a mound on a large plate surrounded by vegetables.

Italian Rice Balls
Serves eight big Italians

Ingredients
2½ cups water
1 cup Arborio rice
¼ cup Romano cheese, grated
3 tablespoons fresh
parsley, finely minced
¼ cup tomato sauce
(homemade if you have it)
¼ cup mozzarella
cheese, diced
salt and pepper to taste
½ cup prosciutto (ham), diced
3 large eggs
2 cups fresh breadcrumbs
groundnut oil, for deep frying

M e t h o d
Bring 2½ cups (600 ml) water to
boil, in a saucepan, and add rice.
Cook for 15 minutes, drain and
transfer to a bowl. Beat one egg and
add to the rice, along with the
Romano cheese, parsley, 2 tablespoons (30 ml) tomato sauce, salt
and pepper. Mix well and chill in
the fridge for 15 minutes.

In another bowl mix the mozzarella,
prosciutto and remaining tomato
sauce. Flour your hands and divide
the rice into eight portions and roll
into a ball about the size of a small
orange.

Poke a hole in the ball with your
finger and put about 1½ tablespoons (20ml) of the mozzarella
mixture into the hole. Reshape and
smooth the rice ball to close
the hole.

Beat the remaining eggs in a shallow
bowl and spread breadcrumbs out
on a plate. Roll the rice balls in
egg, coating well, then in breadcrumbs and coat evenly. Let sit for
45 minutes.

In a heavy pan or deep fryer, heat
oil to 375°F. Fry the rice balls until
golden. Drain on a paper towel and
serve hot.

Mushroom and Corn Roulade (v)
Serves 4

Ingredients

Roulade:
2 oz margarine
4 tablespoons wholemeal plain flour
6 fl oz ml milk
3 free-range eggs, separated
4 oz canned creamed corn

Mushroom Filling
3 fl oz vegetable stock or water
3 tablespoons thick sour cream or natural yoghurt
2 tablespoons chopped fresh basil
½ oz vegetable margarine
6 oz mushrooms, finely chopped
1 onion, finely chopped
1 tablespoon plain flour

Method
Preparing the roulade:
First, melt the margarine in a saucepan, stir in the flour and cook for 1 minute. Gradually blend in the milk and cook over a medium heat, stirring frequently, until the mixture boils and thickens. Whisk in the egg yolks and corn. Then whisk the egg whites until stiff peaks form and gently fold through corn mixture. Spread the mixture into a lightly greased and greased-paper-lined 25 x 30 cm (10 x 12 inch) Swiss roll tin. Bake at 220°C/425°F/Gas Mark 7 for 15 – 20 minutes or until puffed and golden.

To make the filling:
Whisk together the stock, sour cream and basil. Melt the margarine in a saucepan, add the mushrooms and onion and cook for 5 minutes or until the onion softens. Add the flour and cook for 1 minute. Gradually stir in the stock mixture and cook over a medium heat, stirring constantly until the mixture boils and thickens.

Turn the roulade onto a wire rack covered with a clean tea towel and remove the paper. Quickly spread with warm filling and gently roll up from the short side, with the help of the tea towel. Serve with lightly steamed vegetables – I recommend broccoli, carrots and potatoes.

Grilled Pesto Lamb with Bruschetta

Serves ten culinary queens

Ingredients

3 cups loosely packed fresh basil leaves (about 2 bunches)

⅓ cup pine nuts (Pignoli)

⅓ cup grated Parmesan cheese

3 tablespoons olive oil

2 tablespoons lemon juice

¾ teaspoon salt

2 garlic cloves

3 pounds boneless lamb leg

Bruschetta (see below)

basil sprigs, for garnish

Method

Prepare pesto: In a food processor with the knife blade attached or in blender at medium speed, blend basil leaves, pine nuts, Parmesan cheese, olive oil, lemon juice, salt, and garlic until well blended. Pour the pesto into a large baking dish; add lamb, turning to coat. Place the lamb under the grill over medium heat, reserving any pesto remaining in the dish. Cook the lamb for 20 to 25 minutes for medium-rare or until of desired 'doneness', brushing with the reserved pesto and turning the lamb occasionally. Remove the lamb to a cutting board. Cut the lamb into serving pieces. Serve with Bruschetta if you like. Garnish with basil sprigs.

Bruschetta

1 medium-sized tomato

1 medium-sized cucumber

1 tablespoon olive oil

2 teaspoons lemon juice

¼ teaspoon black pepper

¼ cup olive paste

crusty white bread

Method

About 20 minutes before serving, seed and coarsely chop the tomato. Peel and coarsely chop the cucumber. In a bowl, mix tomato, cucumber, 1 tablespoon olive oil, 2 teaspoons lemon juice and ¼ teaspoon ground black pepper. Cut the ends off a loaf of bread and slice the remaining loaf diagonally into ¼-inch-thick slices. Under a grill on medium heat, toast bread slices until golden, turning once. Spread the toast slices with olive paste; top with the tomato mixture. Makes 10 accompaniment servings.

Watercress Flan
(v)
Serves four health freaks

Ingredients

To make 6 oz wholemeal
shortcrust pastry:
4 oz wholemeal flour
2 oz oats
pinch salt
1½ oz margarine
1½ oz white
vegetable fat

Filling:
1 oz margarine
1 bunch spring onions,
trimmed, washed and
chopped
2 bunches watercress, washed
and roughly chopped
2 medium eggs
¼ pt natural yoghurt
2 tablespoons milk
4 teaspoons salt
¼ teaspoon ground
black pepper
1 teaspoon fresh parsley
40 oz vegetarian
Cheddar cheese, grated

Method

Pre-heat the oven to 200°C. Roll
out the pastry and use to line an 8
in flan ring. Cover with greaseproof
paper and a weight (dried beans are
good) and bake for 10–15 minutes.

Melt the margarine in a saucepan
and gently fry the spring onions for
2–3 minutes. Add the watercress,
cover and cook over a low heat for a
further 2–3 minutes. Beat the eggs
with the yoghurt, milk, salt, black
pepper and parsley. Place the watercress and spring onions in the bottom of the flan case, sprinkle with
the cheese and pour over the egg and
yoghurt mixture. Bake for 25 – 30
minutes, or until firm to the touch.
Serve hot or cold with a salad or
fresh vegetables.

Shepherd's Pie
Serves six shepherds

Ingredients

7 medium potatoes
(about 2 lb)

1½ lb medium-size
mushrooms

1 lb carrots

1 large celery stalk

1 medium-sized onion

¾ lb extra lean
minced beef

½ teaspoon dried
thyme leaves

olive oil

2 teaspoons plain flour

1 cup water

2 tablespoons Worcestershire
sauce

salt

⅔ cup skimmed milk

2 oz butter

⅛ teaspoon pepper

Method

In a large saucepan over high heat, heat the potatoes and enough water to cover to boiling. Reduce the heat to low; cover and simmer 25 to 30 minutes until the potatoes are fork-tender; drain. Meanwhile, cut each mushroom into quarters. Cut carrots into ½-inch chunks. Finely chop celery and onion. In a frying pan over high heat, cook the minced beef, celery, onion, and thyme in olive oil until all juices evaporate and meat is browned, stirring frequently. Remove the meat mixture to a separate plate.

In the same pan over medium-high heat, in olive oil, cook carrots and mushrooms until they are golden brown and the carrots are tender. In a 1-cup measuring cup, mix flour and 1 cup water until blended. Return the meat mixture to a frying pan; stir in the Worcestershire sauce, 1 teaspoon salt and the flour mixture. Over high heat, heat to boiling; boil for 1 minute.

Preheat oven to 425°F. With potato masher, mash the potatoes in a bowl with milk, butter, pepper, and ½ teaspoon salt until smooth.

Spoon the meat mixture into a shallow large casserole dish. Spoon mashed-potato mixture into a decorating bag fitted with a large writing tube (½ inch wide). Pipe mashed-potato mixture over meat mixture in lattice design and around edge of casserole. (Or if you can't be bothered, just slap it on the top.) Bake 10 to 15 minutes until potatoes are golden brown.

Tip
I often put some grated cheese on top of the potato, it adds that little extra tasty spark.

Tina's Spinach Pie (and tsatsiki) (v)

Serves 8 as a starter,
4 as a main course

Ingredients
2 bunches spring onions
olive oil
1 kg (at least) fresh spinach
(with the stalks removed)
bunch watercress (optional)
bunch rocket (optional)
bunch of lamb's lettuce
(optional)
pinch of dill
pinch of nutmeg
100 g feta cheese (cubed)
100 g pine kernels
1 egg (optional)
1 packet filo pastry
(10–15 leaves)(you can find it
in the frozen section in supermarkets – it doesn't keep very
well, so use straight away)

You also need a brush
for the pastry.

Method
Preheat a gas oven to Mark 7. Sauté the onions (chopped finely) in olive oil. In a separate pan, steam the spinach for a minute or so, drain it to remove all the excess water, and throw it in with the onions. Add the rest of the greens, dill and nutmeg, stir, then add the feta and pine kernels. Leave to cool. Brush the base of the oven dish with oil (using your pastry brush). Carefully remove one leaf of the filo pastry and place on the bottom, brush it with oil (otherwise it gets dry and burns), add more leaves until you've used half of the leaves in the packet. Add the spinach mixture and then the rest of the filo leaves, oiling each one in turn. When you've used all the leaves you can cut the top of the pastry with a kitchen knife into nine pieces. Beat the egg and brush it on top if you want. Put into the oven and leave for 45 minutes to one hour (until the pastry gets quite crispy on top).

You can serve this either hot or cold (it actually becomes tastier if you leave it in the fridge for a couple of days). Serve with Tsatsiki and white wine (not retsina because it's disgusting).

T s a t s i k i

This is a traditional Greek dish that people in England try and make, but they don't tend to succeed and it's tragic – so this is the real tsatsiki.

Ingredients

1 medium cucumber
(peeled if you like)

1 tablespoon salt

3 medium garlic cloves,
crushed or chopped

pepper or paprika to taste

3 tablespoons olive oil

1 tablespoon vinegar
(balsamic if you like)

2 tubs strained greek yoghurt
(200 g each)

2 teaspoons fresh dill
(or fresh mint)

M e t h o d

Grate the cucumber in a cheese grater. Put it in a bowl and add the salt on top of it. Place it in the fridge for an hour and the water should come out of the cucumber. Remove the excess water and leave the cucumber in the bowl. Add the crushed garlic, pepper (or paprika), the oil and vinegar, and mix. Add the yogurt, dill (or mint), leave in the fridge for at least an hour so that the garlic flavour can come out. The consistency should then be quite thick.

Serve it cold with the spinach pie (which can be hot or cold). It's excellent for barbecues in the summer but remember it is very garlicky so it's not recommended for hot dates.

Matthew Linfoot's
Pasta à la Eliot
Serves 2

This is a lazy queen recipe - with a kick. My friend Eliot gave me this recipe. He now lives in San Francisco but I still have the taste of Eliot.

Ingredients
pasta
olive oil
½ bottle of passata
sun-dried tomatoes
(butchly chopped)
white wine balsamic vinegar
salt
pepper
dessertspoon sugar
tin tuna
olives
pine nuts
Parmesan cheese

Method
Cook the pasta in boiling water till al dente. When boiled, drain, throw back in the pan with some olive oil (and some of the oil from the sun-dried tomatoes). Add all ingredients except for cheese, stir for 15 minutes and add the Parmesan. Serve it immediately (because it congeals very easily).

Carpaccio di Verdure, con Salsa alla Rucola e Yogurt (v)

(Vegetable carpaccio with a rocket and yogurt sauce)

Serves two pretentious queens

Ingredients

2 large ripe beef tomatoes
1 green tomato
1 avocado
½ small pineapple
1 small white onion
juice of 1 lemon
salt and pepper to taste
3 tablespoons extra virgin olive oil
1 small bunch fresh basil
1 small bunch rocket, chopped
6 oz yoghurt
1 ice cube

Method

Remove the seeds from the tomatoes and dice them. Cut all the other vegetables and the pineapple the same size, mix in a bowl, add the lemon juice, salt and plenty of pepper, 2 tablespoons olive oil, and half the basil, cut up roughly.

Brush 4–5 little bowls or cups with oil, fill with the diced vegetable, and press with the back of the spoon or a glass. Refrigerate until needed. Remove from refrigerator, drain off any liquid that has formed, turn over gently on to a plate, keeping the shape.

Put the yogurt in the blender, with the chopped rocket and the rest of the basil, salt and 1 ice cube. Blend until you get light green smooth sauce. Pour around the mound of vegetables: serve any remaining sauce on the side.

Vegetable Moussaka (v)
Serves four vegetarians

Ingredients
4 lb aubergines
olive oil
1 oz butter
2 onions
3 ripe tomatoes, chopped
1½ pints white sauce
pinch cinnamon
½ lb grated cheese
1 oz butter
3 free-range eggs

Method

Slice half the aubergines and fry until tender in butter and olive oil, drain and set aside. Cut the remaining aubergines, into large chunks, boil in water until softened, peel and chop. Sauté the onions in olive oil until tender and then add the aubergine pulp and the chopped tomatoes.

Stir in 2 tablespoons of the white sauce and add the cinnamon. Line a greased dish with a layer of the fried aubergines, cover with some of the tomato mixture and sprinkle with grated cheese. Alternate these layers using all the fried aubergines but only half of the cheese. Beat the eggs into the remaining white sauce and pour over the dish. Sprinkle with the remaining cheese and bake in a moderate oven for 30–40 minutes, or until golden.

Ally's Sauce aux Jambon Madere (Ham in Madeira Wine Sauce)
Serves 2

Don't serve on a hot day, save for a winter or autumnal evening. It's very rich and easy.

Ingredients

Large pot single cream (14 fl oz)

tin of tomato purée

1 shallot, chopped

fresh tarragon (handful)

fresh chives (handful)

parsley, chopped

glass of madeira wine

1 packet ham (8 pieces)

Method

In a bowl put the cream, tomato purée, shallot and herbs. Mix well and add a wine glass of madeira wine and mix.

Roll the ham into rolls (obviously) and put into a large baking dish. Pour the sauce over the top, shove it into a medium oven for 20 minutes and you're all set. Serve with pasta and a fresh salad.

Paul's Cream Chicken and Layer Salad

When I cook, or rather try to cook, I like to make things that don't take a lot of ingredients and rarely measure things out. The amounts for both of these recipes are 'as much as you can eat or as much as you need'! I learned how to make this from a beautiful Iraqi man I met in Paris when I was there for work.

Cream Chicken

Ingredients:

sliced fresh mushrooms – though canned ones are OK, but drain them

butter, for sautéing

skinless chicken parts I like using boneless chicken thighs myself

whipping cream – use enough to cover the chicken when first poured on.

salt and pepper

Sauté the mushrooms in a skillet with butter until well cooked. Place the chicken over the mushrooms and cook on both sides until the meat turns white. (This is usually a couple of minutes on both sides.) Pour whipping cream over the chicken and mushrooms until just covered and add salt and pepper to taste. Cook over low heat until whipping cream is thickened. Be sure to cook over LOW heat – if you cook it too fast over a higher heat, you end up with chicken floating in what looks like melted butter. (This happened to me once!) Taste sauce from time to time to add more salt or pepper, if needed.

I like to serve it with rice and broccoli. For the rice I add some curry powder to the water first, this adds a wonderful flavour to the dish. For the broccoli, cut up pieces and place in a dish, add a sprinkle of water and lemon juice. Add some capers and a little of the juice from the capers. Cover and microwave until the veggies are cooked.

Layer Salad

I like to make this for big family dinners or for picnics.

Ingredients
lettuce
red onion
cauliflower
grated cheddar cheese
mayonnaise
sugar
bacon

Method
Place a bed of lettuce in a bowl. Cover with a layer of chopped red onions, then a layer of cut up cauliflower, followed by a layer of shredded cheddar cheese. Cover all of this with a layer of mayonnaise and sprinkle a little sugar over the top. Place in the fridge and leave it overnight. Sometime before serving, cook bacon till it is crisp. Crunch up the bacon and toss it on top of the salad. Mix all of these ingredients in well before serving.

Paul's Double-gingered Orange Chicken

Serves 6

Ingredients

6 boneless, skinless chicken breast halves

½ teaspoon salt (optional)

pepper, to taste

olive oil

6 fl oz frozen orange juice, thawed, diluted with 1 juice can water

1 teaspoon minced fresh ginger

1 teaspoon dried ground ginger

½ teaspoon English mustard

2 teaspoons soy sauce

1 teaspoon dried parsley

4 tablespoons slivered almonds

6 oz rice

We sometimes think low-fat, fast and easy are synonymous with tasteless, but with the right combination of ingredients, such a dish can also be quite tasty, as well as elegant. I created this recipe several years ago using some of my favourite ingredients.

Method

Preheat oven to 375°F. Sprinkle chicken with salt and pepper and brown on both sides in a large, non-stick frying pan with the olive oil over medium-high heat, about 3 minutes on each side. Place the chicken in a single layer in a 13 x 9-inch baking pan. In a blender container, combine diluted orange juice, fresh and dry ginger, mustard and soy sauce. Blend for 10 seconds on low speed and pour over chicken. Sprinkle with parsley and almonds. Bake in a preheated oven for 20 minutes. While the chicken is cooking, boil the rice. Serve the chicken with rice, spooning orange sauce over both.

Spinach Pasta Sauce (v)

Serves 2

Having a blender saves huge amounts of time when you're in a rush and people are on their way round for dinner. This is a speciality of mine.

Ingredients
1 cup chopped/ washed/drained spinach
2 tablespoons olive oil
½ cup no-fat plain yoghurt
1 clove crushed garlic
teaspoon basil
1 handful of fresh chopped parsley
juice of one lemon
2 tablespoons crumbled feta cheese

Method
Whirl all the ingredients (except feta cheese) in a blender until chunky-smooth. Add warm water to thin a little, if necessary. Cook pasta until *al dente*. Toss the pasta with a little butter, then add sauce. Mix very thoroughly, add the feta cheese and toss again.

Tina's Chicken Stifado

Serves four strapping butches, three big military boys or six femmes

This is a variation of two or three Greek recipes but it's been queered up a bit. Stifado means the process of cooking in a red tomato sauce with pickling onions. It's usually used for hare or rabbit but I know how squeamish the British are.

Ingredients
1½ lb pickling onions
olive oil
4 lbs chicken pieces
(for a British audience make that boneless breast and thigh pieces. In Greece you just throw in the whole chicken but I know that British people can't take that)
glass of red wine
1 tablespoon tomato purée
1 teaspoon cinnamon
½ teaspoon cloves
1 teaspoon nutmeg
2 bay leaves
1 teaspoon ground cumin
1 small cup balsamic vinegar (expresso size)
salt and pepper

Method
Sauté the onions whole in the oil and sauté the bits of bird until they're all golden brown. Stir in the wine and the tomato purée (diluted in a glass of warm water), and the herbs and spices. Cover and simmer for about 2 hours – keep checking to make sure it doesn't dry up. Then throw in the vinegar, stir in and wait for 5 minutes and add salt and pepper. Serve with basmati rice.

Goat's Cheese Torta with Pesto and Sun-dried Tomatoes (v)

Serves 4

Ingredients

6 oz goat cheese

4 oz cream cheese

8 cloves garlic (crushed)

salt and pepper (optional)

½ cup pesto (at least)

½ cup chopped up fine oil-packed sun-dried tomatoes, (including 1 – 2 teaspoons of the marinade)

fresh herbs to garnish,

such as branches of thyme, oregano, rosemary, parsley

sliced French bread

Method

Mix the goat cheese and cream cheese, and add the garlic. Check the taste. Add salt and black pepper if you want. Line a small glass bowl (about 2 – 3 cups) with plastic wrap. Put about ⅓ of the goat-cheese mix into the bowl. Top this with the pesto. Put another 1/3 of the goat cheese mix on top of this. Put the sun-dried tomatoes on this. Top with the rest of the cheese. Put plastic wrap over the top of this. Refrigerate for at least 2 hours, and up to four days. To serve, invert bowl on a serving dish. Carefully remove the plastic wrap. Decorate with the fresh herbs (this is the creative part – any amount of high-school frustrated art can come into play).

Heat the baguettes in the oven until crispy and serve in slices with the Torta.

Chicken and Pasta
Serves 4

Chicken with a bit of a kick. If you hate the taste of curry powder then don't include it but it may taste better than you think.

Ingredients

4 small skinless, boneless chicken-breast halves (about 1 lb)

3 large carrots

1 medium-sized onion

3 cups Farfalle or bow-tie pasta

1oz light corn-oil spread (or butter)

salt

3 tablespoons of water

1½ teaspoons curry powder

1 teaspoon grated peeled ginger

1 x 14 oz can diced tomatoes

1 cup frozen peas, thawed

½ teaspoon sugar

½ cup water

Method

Cut each chicken-breast half cross-wise into 2 or 3 pieces. Cut carrots into 1½ x ¼ inch sticks. Chop the onion. In the saucepan over high heat, boil some water. Add pasta and cook until almost tender; drain and set aside. In non-stick frying pan over medium-high heat, in 1 table-spoon of hot light corn-oil spread, cook chicken and ½ teaspoon salt until the chicken is browned and the juices run clear when chicken is pierced with tip of knife; remove to plate. In the same skillet, add 1 more tablespoon of hot corn-oil spread, cook carrots and onion until browned. Reduce heat to medium. Add 3 tablespoons water; cover and cook until vegetables are tender, about 5 minutes longer. Stir curry powder and ginger into the skillet with vegetables; cook 1 minute. Stir in pasta, chicken, tomatoes with their liquid, peas, sugar, ½ teaspoon salt, and ½ cup water; over high heat, heat to boiling. Reduce heat to low; simmer, uncovered, until the pasta is tender and the mixture heats through, about 3 minutes.

Lamb Chops Supreme with Asparagus

Serves 6

Method

Season the lamb with salt and pepper to taste. In a small bowl, mix the mustard powder, teaspoon water and garlic and coat the lamb chops with the liquid. Then heat the butter in a frying pan and sauté the chops on a high heat until they're brown on both sides, about 3 to 5 minutes per side for pink lamb.

Set aside on a warm plate.

Ingredients

6 lamb chops, lean and trimmed of all fat (boneless chicken breast can be substituted in this recipe)

salt and pepper, to taste

1 teaspoon dry mustard

1 teaspoon water

2 cloves garlic, finely chopped

1 tablespoon butter

The Mint Sauce

Ingredients

1 tablespoon cold butter

1 teaspoon finely chopped shallots

½ cup finely chopped mint

1 cup champagne, white wine or chicken stock

pinch of sugar (optional)

Method

Melt half the butter in a pan and sauté the shallots until tender. Add the mint and stock. Simmer sauce for 3 minutes. Add the remainder of the cold butter and the pinch of sugar. Serve immediately, by drizzling the sauce over warm lamb chops.

Asparagus with Toasted Pecans

Ingredients
½ lemon
1 lb fresh asparagus
1 cup of pecan nuts, chopped medium fine
2 tablespoons olive oil (or butter)
¼ teaspoon grated nutmeg
salt and pepper to taste

Method
Fill a pot large enough for the asparagus to lay flat with water and bring to the boil. Add the lemon juice and the asparagus and cook for 3 to 5 minutes only. Remove the asparagus from the heat and immediately plunge into cold water to stop the cooking process. Set aside. In a frying pan over a high heat, toast the pecan pieces, shaking the pan and stirring with a wooden spoon for several minutes – be careful not to burn them. Remove to a plate and set aside.

Add the olive oil (or butter) and nutmeg to a hot skillet and sauté the asparagus for 3 minutes to heat through. Season then roll in chopped pecans and serve next to lamb chops.

Fernando's Stewed Octopus with Potatoes and Chocolate
Serves 4

Ingredients

400 g fresh octopus
(if no octopus use squid)

olive oil, for frying

2 or 3 cloves garlic

2 Spanish onions, finely chopped

1 tablespoon chopped parsley

1 teaspoon white pepper

pinch salt

½ bay leaf

1 branch thyme

1 kg small new potatoes (scrubbed)

1 tablespoon tomato purée

1 cup anisette (preferably dry Spanish anisette – *anisede del moro* – or French anisette, which is clear)

½ l white wine

2 strands saffron

1 oz powdered chocolate (cocoa)

This is an ancient Catalan recipe from the Mediterranean coast. It belonged to my great-grandmother who is something of a mythical figure in my family and she came from a Catalan family who had plantations in Cuba (then a Spanish colony). She came to Spain when she was 15 (with a personal slave called Ramona who looked after her ailing eyes and stayed with her after slaves were liberated), bringing with her all sorts of bizarre recipes. The recipe warns that it's a strong dish and should not be eaten in the evening because it's very heavy, so this is a lunchtime dish. It sounds scandalous but I have made it and it does work – I've cooked it for friends and it's delicious, if a little unusual.

Method

Clean the octopus and boil it in water for a few minutes. Use a fat-bellied pot with a narrow top (preferably terracotta). Drain and put the olive oil in the pot and add the garlic; when the garlic begins to turn golden brown, take it out and keep it separately.

Then add the onions to the oil and fry. When they begin to become translucent, add the octopus, parsley, pepper and salt, ½ bay leaf and a branch of thyme and the potatoes. Stir the pot slowly on a low heat. Add the tomato purée, anisette and half a litre of white wine. Cover the pot and simmer.

Crush the saffron, garlic and cocoa in a pestle and mortar, add a tablespoon of boiling water until it's a thick paste. Add to the stew, cover the pot and stew until the octopus and potatoes are cooked. The recipe literally says 'stew on a low flame until it's stewed'.

Serve by pouring into a large bowl.

Maria Esposito's Traditional Italian Dishes

Basic Spaghetti Tomato Sauce (v)
Serves 4

Ingredients
2 tablespoons olive oil
3–4 cloves garlic (crushed)
2 x 14 oz tins chopped tomatoes
1 tablespoon tomato purée
salt and pepper
bay leaf / oregano / basil (optional)
¼ teaspoon sugar

This recipe has been in our family for a long time. My grandparents were Italian and we got taught how to make spaghetti sauce when I was very young. Saturday night was a huge family meal in our house, much more important than Sunday lunch, and if you were within a mile vicinity of the house you *would* be staying to eat. Mum, even to this day, will start cooking this pasta sauce at about 8.30 in the morning. The house is full of the smell of garlic with this huge pot of sauce – and everyone walks by and dips bits of bread in it.

You don't have to go out and buy Paul Newman's sauce because this recipe is simple, it's just tins of tomatoes and tomato purée. But the secret of it is that you have to let it cook because tomatoes can be very acidic. This is an excellent dish to start in the morning and let stand because it gets better the longer you leave it.

Method

Put the oil in a deep saucepan and add the garlic (keep on a low heat to stop the garlic burning). Add the tomatoes and tomato purée. Raise the heat and bring to the boil, then simmer and add the salt and pepper. If you want to flavour the sauce with herbs, add them in now. Simmer with a lid on and stir occasionally for an hour or so. Once it's started to cook, add the sugar and simmer for a further half hour. Then let it stand for as long as possible. When you're ready to eat, reheat the sauce and serve it with pasta and Parmesan cheese.

Tip

This sauce is also perfect for putting on sandwiches and can be frozen. If you eat meat, then chicken infuses well with the sauce, as does beef, if you part roast it and then boil it in the sauce – and it's beautiful.

Aubergine Parmesan (v)

This recipe uses the tomato sauce (pages 100 – 101) which you could have made the day before.

Ingredients

2 medium aubergines or one great big one

4 large eggs

2 cups of grated Parmesan cheese

salt and pepper

olive oil

½ pint spaghetti sauce

Method

Cut the spiky bit off the end of the aubergines and wash them. Slice them lengthways in very thin strips (a good knife would be a useful thing here). Beat the egg with the Parmesan cheese (add salt and pepper) to make a batter.

Heat the oil in a frying pan, dip the leaves of aubergine in the batter and fry in the olive oil until they're crisp on both sides. When each slice is golden brown, lay it on kitchen towel to remove some of the grease. Once you've cooked all the aubergine, grease a casserole dish. Pour a layer of spaghetti sauce onto the bottom of the dish, add a layer of aubergine, then another layer of spaghetti sauce and some Parmesan. Build up the layers until you've used it all up.

Bake in the oven (Gas Mark 5) for 30 minutes. It's delicious hot but even more delicious cold, served with a salad. In Italy we usually have pasta as a starter, and an ideal dinner party for me would be pasta followed by aubergine Parmesan and a salad.

Tip
Don't bother taking the bitterness from the aubergine by salting it - you don't need to.

Olga Buckley's Spanish Irish Lardons
Serves two hungry women

I was visiting Santiago de Campatella with my girlfriend and it was our first meal there. We noticed a Guinness sign in the medieval square and by chance there was a folk festival going on and Sharon Shannon was singing. So our first meal was a traditional Irish one.

Ingredients
1 onion
400 g petit pois
1 large clove garlic
handful fresh thyme
1 teaspoon cayenne pepper
1 tablespoon tomato purée
200 g diced, smoked lardons
2 tablespoons white wine
lemon juice
salt
pepper

Method
Fry the onion and the garlic and add the thyme when they're translucent. Add the cayenne pepper, tomato purée and the lardons and turn the heat up to full pelt until they're done. Add the white wine, lemon juice, salt and pepper, stir in for 10 minutes. Then add the petit pois – if you can get fresh, good luck to you, but tinned will do. Serve in an earthenware dish.

Christopher's Exquisite Risotto
Serves 4

Ingredients
2 oz butter

3 tablespoons olive oil

1 onion, finely chopped

½ bottle white wine

¾ pint stock (cubes will do)

1 cup (small mug) arborio rice

1 small tin (7 oz) tuna steak
in brine or water

1 small tin (7 oz) sweetcorn
in water

5 tablespoons freshly grated
Parmesan cheese

handful flat parsley,
finely chopped

salt and pepper

This risotto dish is incredibly adapt-able – my particular favourite is the tuna and sweetcorn option because it's extremely easy to make and tastes like it took a colossal amount of effort. The key to a good risotto is the rice – if you haven't got arbo-rio rice (Italian rice that you can get in any Italian deli and most big supermarkets), don't bother making a risotto, as no other rice will do.

Method
Take two saucepans (one large and heavy, one medium for the stock). I use Le Creuset because I'm a snob but any heavy pan will do. In the large pan, heat the butter and oil and fry the onion until it starts to become translucent. In the stock pan, pour in the wine and the stock, gently bring to the boil and keep simmering on a low heat.

Add the rice to the onion and stir for 2 minutes, then add a ladle of the stock and wine and let the risot-to mixture absorb it. Repeat this until all the stock has been absorbed – stir occasionally to ensure that the rice doesn't stick. Once all the stock has been absorbed, add the tuna and the sweetcorn (remove the excess water from the cans first). Break up the chunks of tuna and mix well with the rice. Then add the Parmesan and the parsley.

Season with salt and freshly milled pepper and serve with a crisp white wine (I'd go for a Chenin Blanc or a Pinot Grigio).

This risotto recipe can be adapted in several ways – it's particularly good with button mushrooms, tomatoes, courgettes and garlic or with left-over chicken.

Beef and Cheese Tortilla Casserole
Serves 6

Ingredients

2 lbs lean ground beef or turkey

1 medium onion, chopped

2 teaspoons instant coffee (optional)

1 teaspoon salt

3 teaspoons chilli powder

¼ teaspoon pepper

3 or 4 x 8 oz cans tomato sauce

12 corn tortillas

3 oz cream cheese

½ cup water

2 cups grated Cheddar cheese

12 ripe olives, pitted and sliced

Method

Brown the meat and onion in a frying pan. Add the coffee, salt, chilli powder, pepper and 2 cans of tomato sauce. Spread each tortilla with cream cheese (use it all). Place a couple of spoonfuls of meat on each tortilla and fold. Place in a greased 9 x 13 inch dish. Pour remaining mixture into any spaces in the dish. Then pour the remaining 1 – 2 cans of sauce and ½ cup water (2 cans for moister casserole) onto the tortilla dish. Sprinkle with cheese and sliced olives. Cover with foil and bake at 375°F for 25 minutes.

Chicken Niçoise
Serves 4

Ingredients

3 large eggs

1 lb 4 oz roasted chicken-breast halves

2 x 14 oz cans whole new potatoes

8 oz French green beans

4 medium-sized tomatoes

¼ cup pitted black olives

1 medium-seized red onion

olive oil

¼ cup lemon juice

2 teaspoons drained capers

2 teaspoons sugar

½ teaspoon Dijon mustard

¼ teaspoon salt

¼ teaspoon ground black pepper

½ head Cos lettuce

½ head green lettuce

Method

Hard-boil the eggs. Meanwhile, remove and discard the skin and bones from the chicken-breast halves; cut meat into ½-inch-wide strips. Drain potatoes and cut in half, if large. Boil the French beans for 5 minutes in a separate pan. Cut tomatoes into ¼-inch-thick slices. Thinly slice the olives. Cut the red onion crosswise into thin slices; separate slices into rings. In frying pan over medium-high heat, in 1 tablespoon hot olive oil, cook onion rings, stirring occasionally, until tender; set aside.

In small bowl, with wire whisk or fork, mix lemon juice, capers, sugar, mustard, salt, and pepper until blended. Gradually add ¼ cup olive oil, whisking constantly, until the dressing is blended.

To serve, remove the shells from the hard-boiled eggs. Cut each egg into quarters. Arrange the lettuce on a large platter with the chicken strips in centre. Arrange potatoes, beans, tomato slices, eggs, and sautéed onion around chicken. Sprinkle with sliced ripe olives. Drizzle salad with dressing; toss to serve.

Desserts

Baked Bananas
Serves 4

Though this may sound a little less than sophisticated, it's easy to make and extremely tasty. Good to round off a dinner party when you've probably drunk too much wine to concentrate on anything too complicated and arduous.

Ingredients
4–6 bananas (4 if really large)
2 oz butter
2 oz light muscovado sugar
1 teaspoon cinnamon
1 tablespoon rum or brandy

Method
Slice the bananas into an ovenproof dish. Melt the butter and stir in the sugar, cinnamon and rum or brandy. Pour over the bananas. Cover the dish with foil and then bake in a preheated oven at Gas Mark 4 for 15 – 20 minutes.

Serve with cream or ice-cream.

Tip
These are particularly good cooked on the barbecue. Just wrap up the bananas, with the other ingredients, in silver foil and cook for 10 minutes.

Classic Bread and Butter Pudding

Serves 4

There's nothing like home cooking. This pudding makes up in taste what it lacks in glamour.

Ingredients
6 – 8 slices thin bread, well buttered with the crusts removed
4 oz dried fruit
Grated rind of 1 lemon or orange
2 oz brown sugar
½ pint milk
1 large egg.

Method

Butter a shallow 1½ pint pie dish well. Cut each slice of bread into three and arrange half the bread, butter side down, in the dish. Cover with most of the fruit, lemon or orange rind, half the sugar and then top with the remaining bread and butter, butter side uppermost. Sprinkle with the rest of the fruit, lemon rind and sugar.

Blend the milk and egg and strain ove the pudding. Leave to soak for at least half an hour, but longer is better.

Bake at Gas Mark 4 for 40 minutes or until puffy, pale golden brown and firm.

Scottish Laura's Grape Fromage Frais and Sherry Gouk
Serves 4

Ingredients

1 lb grapes (seedless, it doesn't matter what colour)

3 sherry glasses of sherry

2½ tablespoons soft brown sugar

large tub fromage frais

Very quick and easy – ideal for communal dinner parties if you can't be arsed to make anything proper. I always believe in putting alcohol in my recipes because if it goes disasterously wrong you can just polish off the rest of the bottle. I also particularly enjoy preparing the desserts at a dinner party, because by the time it gets to the last course people tend to be so drunk that all they want is something sweet.

Method

Cut the grapes in half and put in a bowl, add sherry and 1½ tablespoons sugar, bung in in the fridge for an hour and let it get cold. Take out of the fridge and mix in a big tub of fromage frais and another tablespoon of brown sugar. Slop it into some bowls and feed to unsuspecting people.

Scottish Laura's Nectarine Special

Serves as many as you want

Ingredients

one nectarine (or peach) for each person

butter (knobs of)

soft brown sugar (teaspoons of)

fromage frais or double cream

Method

Score round the sides of the nectarines and twist, take the stone out. Where the stone used to live, put a knob of butter, topped with a teaspoon of brown sugar. Whack it in the oven at 150°C for 20 minutes. Get it out and pop it in bowls. What happens is that the nectarines go soft and the middle treacles up nicely. Then add two dollups of cream or fromage frais depending on how healthy you feel.

You can use peaches but I prefer nectarines because I'm not very fond of peach skin.

Peter Tatchell's Orange Pancakes
Serves two gay activists

This recipe was a traditional Sunday morning in bed treat for one of my ex-boyfriends, but also makes an excellent dessert.

Ingredients

Batter:
4 oz plain flour
2 oz raw or muscovado sugar
pinch of salt
1 beaten egg
½ pint milk
1oz melted butter
1 grated orange rind
butter for frying

Topping:
Juice of 3 medium oranges
grated rind of 1 large orange
½ teaspoon crushed
dried mint

Method
Blend the batter ingredients together to create a runny batter mix. Add a little extra milk, if necessary. Pour a small amount of the batter into a hot, well-buttered frying pan – tilting the pan back and forth to make the pancake as thin as possible. When brown, flip the pancake over to cook the other side. Stack the pancakes on a warmed plate and sprinkle a little additional muscovado sugar between each layer. When the pancakes are cooked, return them to the frying pan on a low heat. Mix together the orange juice, orange rind and mint, and pour over the pancakes. When the orange juice is hot but not boiling, remove from the heat and serve with an additional sprinkling of muscovado sugar, if desired.

Vivian Nelson's Marshmallow Dream

Serves several sweet-toothed lesbians

My mother taught me this recipe which I would ideally serve to a gastronomically susceptible woman.

Ingredients
8 oz evaporated milk
1½ cups sugar
margarine
flavour chips (chocolate, chocolate/mint, and peanut butter work best; use less than a full bag for chocolate ones)
1 teaspoon vanilla essence
13 oz jar marshmallow creme

Method

Pour the evaporated milk into a saucepan, add the sugar and heat to bubbling, stirring all the while. Allow to bubble for 6 minutes. Add vanilla (watch out for the splash!!). Next add the marshmallow creme. Stir well (if you have carpal tunnel, get assistance).

Add flavour chips of choice (amount varies with taste desire) and stir well. Pour out onto foil or marble and spread thinly. Wait, then sample when your mouth won't get burned.

Tip
Make your first batch with no bystanders: if it doesn't work, no one will know. If it does you can eat all you want, then tell them after you have arranged the rest so they don't know how much there was to start with.

Jim and David's Best Lemon Meringue Pie in the World

Serves two hungry beefcakes

Ingredients

1¼ cups sugar

1½ cups boiling water

6 tablespoons cornstarch

2 lemons (grate the rind, and squeeze for the juice)

2 eggs, separated

1 baked pie shell

¼ teaspoon cream of tartar

2 tablespoons sugar for meringue

Method

Dissolve the sugar in boiling water. Mix the cornstarch in a small amount of water; stir into the sugar water until thickened. Mix in the lemon juice and grated rind. Then mix in the beaten egg yolks. Stir well – cool. Pour cooled mix into baked pie shell.

Meringue:

Beat the egg whites until somewhat stiff, adding ¼ teaspoon cream of tartar. Beat in sugar; spread on the pie, being careful to seal the edge. Bake at 350°F 12 for 15 minutes, or until brown. Cool before slicing so the filling will be set!

Crème Brûlée
Serves 8

Posh name, posh dessert, but if you're attempting to wow with your culinary capabilities, it's a good choice.

Ingredients

1 quart
whipping cream

8 egg yolks

1 cup soft
brown sugar

1 tablespoon
vanilla essence

Method

Heat the cream in a saucepan on a low heat until tiny bubbles form around the edges. In a large mixing bowl, beat the egg yolks and sugar until pale and creamy. Add the vanilla essence. Gradually add the cream to the egg and sugar mixture while mixing.

Pour the mixture carefully into eight 4 oz custard dishes (like everyone just has custard dishes lying around! – small bowls will do for the rest of us).

Place the dishes in a pan with warm water (bain-marie). Bake at 350°F for 45 minutes. Whack them into the fridge. You can do all the basic preparation in advance.

Just before serving, sprinkle top with 1 tablespoon (15 ml) sugar and bake for 5 to 10 minutes more or until golden brown in colour.

Chill and serve.

Tip
Don't keep the bowls too long in the refrigerator once you have glazed them with sugar, as the sugar will melt. It is better to keep it at room temperature just before serving.

Dinner Parties

an eyecatching presentation is half the battle

STEVE PEARSON'S CLASSIC DINNER PARTY
6 people

The secret of a good dinner party is organization and you should enjoy the dinner party as much as your guests do. There's no point in having a dinner party you don't enjoy. Diversity is also key. Cooking for me is trial and error, I don't like being too specific about my recipes.

Fried Brie (v)

Ingredients
2oz Brie per portion
parsley-seasoned flour
1 egg
sunflower oil
breadcrumbs (with chopped fresh coriander)
redcurrant jelly
lime juice (1½ limes)

Method
Coat the Brie portions a day in advance if possible, then fry in sunflower oil till brown and serve on a base of warmed redcurrant jelly. Squeeze on the lime juice and decorate with slices of lime.

Drink with a dry crisp wine such as a Chablis, a Chardonnay ... or a sparkling Sans Mieur would be quite wonderful.

Tip
It's always best to put the sauce on the base of the dish – the last thing you want to do is to have too many flavours.

Chicken Parcels

These chicken parcels are easy to make and taste fantastic – the spinach keeps all the juices in the parcel so that the meat is quite tender and succulent.

Ingredients
6 boned, skinned chicken breasts
6 oz Stilton cheese
6 spinach leaves
puff pastry

Method

Slit each chicken breast lengthways and insert 1 oz of stilton. Lightly blanch the spinach leaves and wrap around the chicken breasts. Buy a packet of puff-pastry (frozen will do) and roll into thin squares. Place each wrapped chicken breast in the puff pastry and fold to make a parcel. Place these in the oven at 180°C for 25 minutes.

Serve with an egg or herb sauce. For the egg sauce, make a basic white sauce (flour, butter, milk, mustard) and add a chopped hard-boiled egg to the finished sauce. A white sauce is extremely versatile – should you want this recipe to be spiced up a bit, why not add a teaspoon of curry paste (bought in a jar) to it.

Tip
Much of this can be prepared the day before and put in the fridge to ensure that your dinner guests can be attended to at all times.

Caramelized Carrots

This is a fantastic way to turn peas and carrots into something special. I guarantee that if you have these at a dinner party, everyone will ask what you've done to them – it's always a success.

Ingredients
1½ lb carrots
8–10 teaspoons sugar
1 oz butter
cup of frozen peas

Method

Chop the carrots into batons and add enough water to just about cover them. Add the sugar and butter. When the carrots are nearly cooked, add a few frozen peas to them. By this time the water will have reduced sufficiently to form a sticky resin. Turn the peas and carrots in this resin.

Potato Nests

To serve with the chicken, a nice white potato dish will contrast nicely.

Ingredients
potatoes
fresh nutmeg
1 egg yolk or cream
chopped onion
chopped tomato

Mash enough potatoes for six people with some fresh nutmeg and an egg yolk or maybe some cream if you're not too worried about your weight. Pipe the potato into nests on a baking tray with a cavity in the middle of each one. In the middle of the nests, add a teaspoon or so of chopped onion and tomato (lightly fried). Place the baking tray in the oven for a few minutes until the potato nests are crisp.

As far as wine goes for this recipe, you could either stick with white, or a light red wine such as a Burgundy or a Beaujoulais or a Cote de Beaume.

LYNN AND SARAH'S VEGETARIAN BANQUET FOR 10 ON A BABY BELLING (v)

This is an international banquet. It's a summer meal and a joy for all to partake of.

Ingredients

several ripe avocados (you have to be very careful about the consistency of the fruit, soft, yet solid)

mozzarella (as many packets as your guests can eat)

loads of plum tomatoes (grown for flavour)

500 g sweet cherry tomatoes

Kiwi & Rasberry Vinaigrette:

2 kiwi fruit

4 tablespoons balsamic vinegar

4 tablespoons raspberry vinegar

4 tablespoons walnut oil

4 tablespoons olive oil

1 heaped teaspoon grain mustard

squirt lemon juice

twist black pepper

olives or grapes, to garnish

Simple Tricolore with Textured Dressing

Some people prefer the buffalo mozzarella but I find that tastes a bit strong so I've gone for Traditional Italian. I think a good starter should tickle the taste buds, not be too heavy. Presentation is ⅝ of the battle – if it looks nice your guests are going to want to eat it. This starter is particularly good for Baby Belling users as it involves no cooking whatsoever, leaving both of my rings free for the main course.

Method

Slice the avocados, mozzarella and tomatoes finely and arrange artistically on a huge plate. Pulp the kiwi fruit (having peeled and cored it) with the back of a teaspoon. (The exotic fruit section in your average supermarket is getting more and more exciting by the day and you could even try papaya.) Then mix the kiwi pulp, vinegars, oils, mustard, lemon juice and pepper briskly in a jar. Pour the vinaigrette over the salad, garnish with olives (or grapes if you can't get hold of any olives) and serve with a light crisp dry sparkling wine.

Mushroom Melody

We move to south-east Asia for the main course, for a coconut and mushroom curry. I feel that one of the huge misconceptions about vegetarian food is that it has to be without texture, and each one of these types of mushrooms has its own individual texture.

Ingredients
2 tablespoons sunflower oil
2 blocks tofu
soy sauce
500 g shiitake mushrooms
500 g brown-backed mushrooms
500 g large garden mushrooms
500 g oyster mushrooms
(I call these labia mushrooms because of their texture)
100 g coconut block
large tin coconut milk
2 sweet peppers
500 g baby aubergines
300 g baby sweetcorn
small packet peanuts
2 tablespoons peanut butter (sugarless)
half teaspoon lemon grass (dried)
pinch chilli powder
half teaspoon dried ginger
rice, to serve

Method
Take a large wok (always good for large events), add the sunflower oil and fry the tofu (with some soy sauce) until the tofu's slightly browned at the edges. Then add in the mushrooms (saving the oyster until last as they're the most tender). Dilute the coconut block with half a pint of warm water and add that and the coconut cream. Stir for a couple of minutes, add in the rest of the ingredients, boil and simmer for 15 minutes. Meanwhile, on the other ring, boil enough rice for your guests – I recommend a cup per person, serve together and drink with a full bodied red, like a Cabernet Sauvignon.

Exotic Fruit Surprise

Basically go to your nearest supermarket and raid the exotic fruit section for whatever they have – the more ridiculous the better. I'm particularly partial to sharon fruits, purely for the name. Slice up all the fruit you have and serve on huge plates to your hungry guests.

ROSALIND HABER'S MEAL FOR THE JEWISH FALLEN VEGETARIAN
Serves 6

One of my greatest sources of joy is sitting around a table with friends, eating, drinking and talking. And I love to cook. This I learned by watching my mother and grandmother. If I asked how much of something to put in the recipe I'd get a bemused look and a shrug and told 'a bit of this and a bit of that, bibbeles and schmibbeles'. Food was measured in pinchfuls and fistfuls and the word 'recipe' did not exist. That was too formal – you just felt it and, of course, tasted it. One would occasionally have a peep at the culinary bible, Florence Greenberg, but that was not to copy but, in true Jewish tradition, to interpret. I shall spare you the angst and give you a few specific measurements. But if the mood takes you, interpret.

So let's feel our way through Chicken Soup with Kneidle, Latkes with Sour Cream and Israeli Salad.

The Chicken Soup

Now with the chicken soup you know we are talking about a total existential experience. A bit tough on the chicken and a serious dilemma for many a vegetarian Jew. But as we know, laws and traditions are up for challenge.

Ingredients
1 large onion
some carrots
1 courgette
some celery – the leaves are nice too
a few chopped cloves of garlic
fresh parsley
salt and white pepper, to taste
bay leaf (optional)
1 chicken, preferably a boiler (which is an old bird, so at least you know it lived a long life) and if it's got its giblets, so much the better
chicken stock cube (if you're feeling insecure)

Method
Fry the onion till golden and throw in the carrots, courgette, celery, garlic, parsley and the salt and white pepper to taste. You're welcome to toss in a bay leaf if you like.

Put the chicken in and cover with water and bring to the boil. Simmer and simmer, and taste and taste. If you're worried that it will taste bland, crumble in a chicken stock cube and don't tell a soul.

I like to cool it down and let the fat, or the schmaltz, rise to the top and skim it off. This stops the soup being oily and you can reassure the health conscious that their arteries will not clog up at the first spoonful.

The Kneidle

These are luft-kneidle or cloud matzo meal dumplings. I prefer these to the ordinary ones as they are lighter and any effort to get lighter in Ashkenazi Jewish food can only be a plus.

You can also eat kneidle as a side dish or stuff them with chopped meat or onion before boiling them.

Ingredients

6 oz medium matzo meal (which you can get in most decent supermarkets)

a generous ¼ pint of water

1 teaspoon of salt

a sprinkle of cinnamon or nutmeg, or ginger

3 eggs

6 tablespoons of oil (you're right – this is not sponsored by the Heart Foundation)

Method

Mix the matzo meal with the water, salt and spice. Beat the eggs and add them to the mix with the oil. To make sure the kneidle will be light and fluffy, put the mix in the fridge for about 4–6 hours first.

Form the mix into small balls and put them into the soup, a few at a time to avoid squashing them. Cook for a minimum of half an hour, and longer if you like.

The Latkes or Raw Potato Pancakes

Traditionally these are eaten at Chanukkah but I think one should keep in practice the rest of the year.

Ingredients
6 potatoes
1 onion
½ teaspoon bicarbonate of soda
salt and pepper, to taste
2 oz flour
2 eggs
corn oil

Method

Finely grate the potato and onion. Mix with the bicarbonate of soda and drain off any liquid. Then mix in the rest of the ingredients. Heat the oil in a pan. You're not exactly deep frying but you need a goodly amount to get the latke crisp. Drop a small handful (the size of a tablespoon) of the batter into the hot oil and fry until golden on the outside. Turn once and do the other side. Some people like to make them bigger, so choose your size.

Latkes can be served with sour cream, apple sauce or cinnamon and sugar.

The Israeli Salad

Ingredients
cucumber
tomatoes
juice of ½ lemon
a good light olive oil
salt
fresh dill
These are the fundamentals, but if you want to add anything else, such as red peppers or spring onions, feel free

In Israel this simple salad is ubiquitous. Luckily it is delicious, otherwise the visitor would start hallucinating this brightly coloured dish.

Unlike the chicken soup, with its legendary cure-all properties, this dish is actually very healthy, although it is perhaps less fundamentally satisfying.

Method

Chop up the cucumber and as many tomatoes as you want. Mix in the lemon juice, a pouring of olive oil, a goodly amount of salt to taste and the chopped dill. And eat. Enjoy!

AAMIR'S CLASSIC INDIAN DISHES
(All recipes serve 4)

If you speak to any Indian they will tell you that most Indian food you get in Indian restaurants here is nothing like Indian food. This seems to be for two reasons; firstly they seem to cut corners on most dishes, so if they have anything slightly complicated they just don't bother. They rarely use fresh herbs or spices and they just cook the sauce in a big pot separately from the meat and then add more or less chilli depending on what you order. This is totally different from the way it's made in India, where the meat's always cooked with the sauce like a stew.

Secondly there are all these strange concoctions which are complete English inventions. 'Vindaloo' means beef and potatoes – so a prawn vindaloo is a crazy concept, like asking for prawn-flavoured roast chicken. And when dishes are described as 'creamy', it's bizarre because cream does not exist in India – cooking is either done with yoghurt or with condensed milk for desserts. My parents are from northern India – a little village called Arzanger near Banares, 100 miles north of Nepal – and are Muslims, so they do eat meat but 80 per cent of India is vegetarian. The following recipes are from my mother and I grew up on them.

Aamir's Chicken Korma

The most important thing in the sauce is 'browning onions'. It's a very difficult thing to do but incredibly important to get the rich dark velvety sauce. You have to slice them finely and fry them in oil on a very low heat until they're evenly browned – and that really does mean brown, like the colour of brown hair. It's very difficult to ensure that the onions don't get burnt. The ideal way to cook them is so that they're crispy but not burnt.

Ingredients

2 onions finely chopped

oil, for cooking

2 teaspoons cumin seeds

4–5 black peppercorns

2 cloves

3 black and 4–5 green cardamom pods

dalchini (couple of inches)

1 small chicken, boned and the flesh cut into chunks

3 cloves garlic, crushed

1 inch of ginger (finely chopped)

2 red chillies (optional)

1 small tub yoghurt

Method

Brown the onions in enough oil to cover the bottom of the pan (you can have as much oil as you want – oily food isn't a problem for Indian people). On a high heat add the cumin seeds, and the seeds will pop in the hot oil. Add the peppercorns, cloves, cardamom pods (I recommend you go out and buy these because they've got a fantastic rich smoky flavour) and dalchini (cinnamon sticks). Mix together in a pan. Once it's been thoroughly mixed and the spices are heated through in the hot oil, scoop the dry spice mixture out of the pan and put on a plate on the side (it doesn't matter if a few seeds remain in the pan).

Take the chicken and throw it into the oil to seal (until it's completely white and bloodless). Add the garlic, ginger and whole red chillies. Lower the heat and stir, mixing until the garlic's cooked and the chicken's coated. Meanwhile, take the dried spice mixture and crush the onions and the spices as finely as possible. Take a small tub of yoghurt, whip it until it becomes smooth and mix the dried spices into it. Add the yoghurt mixture to the pan (with the chicken in) and stir. If you want a thinner sauce just add water, or if you want a spicier sauce you can add garam masala, just sprinkle it on at the end. Cover and simmer for 10–15 minutes. Serve with basmati rice or naan bread.

Mince and Potatoes

This is an everyday dish that kids have when they come home from school. It's a home dish and not something you'd serve on a rather special occasion.

Ingredients
2 onions, finely chopped
oil, for cooking
3 cloves garlic, crushed
1 inch ginger, chopped
1 teaspoon turmeric
2 small red chillies
1 teaspoon garam masala
1 teaspoon cumin seeds
3 black cardamoms
2 bay leaves
1 lb lamb mince
2 tomatoes
cup of peas (or 4 smallish potatoes, chopped and peeled)
handful fresh coriander, chopped
2 green chillies, chopped

Method

Fry the onions in enough oil to cover the bottom of the pan, add the garlic, ginger, turmeric, red chillies, garam masala, cumin, black cardamoms and bay leaves. Stir well, it should smell very pungent. Add the lamb mince and mix it in. If you can get halal mince it is better because it's less bloody as the blood has been drained, and therefore the taste is less gamey; Indians prefer this sort of flavour. Mix thoroughly. Continue stirring, breaking up all the lumps of meat until it's browned and fried through. Turn the heat down, add a couple of tablespoons of water and leave covered on a low heat for 10 minutes (being careful not to dry it out). Add the tomatoes and stir, then add the peas or potatoes. Add the coriander, green chillies and three tablespoons water, close lid and simmer. Leave until the vegetables are cooked (4 minutes peas and 15 minutes potatoes). Serve.

Ingredients
2 lb floury potatoes
1 tablespoon salt
2 green chillies, finely chopped
small bunch coriander
ground cumin
juice of ½ lemon
1 small onion, chopped
black pepper
peas
garlic
ginger
oil, for frying

Potato Kebabs (v)

They're quite unusual and can be served as a special dish.

Boil and mash the potatoes, add the salt, chillies, coriander, 2 teaspoons ground cumin, lemon juice, onion and lots of ground black pepper. Mix it together and add salt to taste. Take some peas and fry them in garlic, ginger and cumin. Add them to the mixture and then flatten and divide it up. Dip in flour and shallow fry in oil.

ingredients
12 oz wholemeal flour
¼ teaspoon salt
1¼ tablespoons softened ghee
1 teaspoon cumin seeds
1 teaspoon onion seeds (colonji)
oil, for frying

Puris

Into the flour, mix the salt and softened ghee. Add the cumin seeds and onion seeds (colonji). Mix in. Add warm water until it becomes soft elastic. Take out, knead for 5–6 minutes. Roll dough into 20 balls. Take each ball and flatten it into thin pancake five inches in diameter – as thin as possible. Deep fry in oil. As each one's frying, press down until they become fluffy globes. Take out and they should be soft.

Hot Coffee

Above all it is essential that you can make a decent cup of coffee. The main advantage of coffee is that it gives you an opportunity to show off all your shiny new equipment. The market is full of delectable coffee-makers, from those classic expresso jugs to sturdy cafetières and, for the techically minded, a cappuccino machine is a must (none of your plastic though, only smart Italian metal will do), and the obligatory coffee grinder.

But it's not just the aesthetic that's important, it's crucial that your coffee tastes like you're an expert.

The ground rules are:

• Never, never, never use instant. Don't be fooled by the advertising, it does *not* taste the same and neither do those little sachets masquerading as cappucinos.
• Never, never, never use any whitener that has not directly come from a cow.
• Adjust your blend (or at least know what your blend is):
>	Breakfast coffee should be light, something like Columbian or Mocha, and filter not expresso. You don't want to give your overnight guests heart attacks from too much caffeine.
>	After-dinner blends cut through the taste of your meal, so use something more adventurous and stronger like Kenyan or Brazilian.
>	For expresso, the best is really 'Lavazza'. You should buy it in bulk or buy the 'Continental' roasts that you see in supermarkets, but you must grind your beans very finely.
• Buy those little expresso cups (they're really cheap from catering stores) just because they look so cute all lined up together.

If you're feeling really creative, try Turkish coffee. It can be delicious although there is also the potential for mess as the bubbling coffee mixture on your stove will permanently coat your hob with thick brown pungent goo if it boils over.

By Steve Pearson

Knowing what wines to have with what kind of food can be tricky. It's often best to just stick to the basic – white wine with fish or chicken, red with red meat and rich vegetarian dishes. At the end of the day the most important thing is that the wine tastes OK, and you can pretty much guarantee that it will if you follow the wine guides in the Sunday papers or check out the reviews of the wines in the larger supermarkets. There is, however, formal etiquette with wine drinking and here's a formal guide:

Apéritif before dining	Dry Sherry - Dry White Wine - Dry Sparkling Wine - Vermouth
Hors d'oeuvres	Dry White Burgundy - Alsace - No wine if using oil and vinegar
Oysters (you should be so lucky)	Muscadet - Dry Sparkling Wine
Shellfish	Alsace - Muscadet - Soave
Fish	Muscadet - Moselle - White Burgundy. If the fish dish has a cream sauce or cheese - Côte de la reine - Sauternes - Rosé d'Anjou

Grills	Claret - Burgundy - Valpolicella
Beef	Claret - Burgundy - Rhône
Pork/Lamb	Claret - Rhône
Poultry	Claret - Hock - Rosé d'Anjou
Sweets	Asti Spumante - Sparkling Hock - Sauternes - Madeira
Cheese	Most red wines - Port
Coffee	Cognac - Port - Madeira

That's the official guide if you're trying to impress, but to be honest wine's very much up to individual taste. The above list asumes that you'll only drink European wine and, as all discerning queers know, Europe's just half the story; Australian Red Wine is dependably palatable (if a little heavy at times) as is South African White.

Tips for pretending to know about wine:

• Invest in big wine glasses.
• Always look at the bottle for at least two minutes. This gives you the opportunity to digest as much information as possible to regurgitate later on.
• Learn as many synonyms for 'fruity' and 'oaky' as is humanly possible to absorb.
• Whack your nose in your glass with a studied intensity and sniff assertively.
• Start sentences with 'I don't know much about wine but' and continue with all the facts that you do know.
• Don't slurp and spit the wine out, it looks silly.
• If you're really posing, invest in a small bottle of dessert wine. It never fails to impress.
• Liberal use of the words 'rich' and 'full-bodied' are useful in connection with red wines, whereas the words 'light' and 'crisp' are useful for whites.
• Drink slowly, pretend to savour every sip.
• If you think your host knows more than you, listen and learn.

• Practise corking techniques and pouring expertise at home before you venture out.

• Never, never, never buy or serve Liebfraumilch, Asti Spumante, British wine or 'low-alcohol'.

• Buy your wine at a good wine store or supermarket before you go out. In most wine stores the staff know their wines, so listen to them and take mental notes. Cheap wine always tastes cheap, and it's embarrassing to see your guests or host wincing with bitter tastes in their mouths.

The Food Chain
Cooking for people with HIV

the secret of successful soufflés? No BUTTER! Use a water-based lubricant instead

People living with HIV often experience periods when the illness renders them housebound. Sometimes they are too weak to cook themselves proper food. In addition, some medication can adversely affect appetite; HIV can also cause severe weight loss, which can be life threatening, as well as reducing the body's ability to deal with other infections. Good food is the best way to get vital nutrients into the system which can help put back lost weight and help the fight against further infection.

In the UK there is a group dedicated to solving this desperate problem, called The Food Chain. I visited the kitchens in Kentish Town, London, where they help prepare and deliver three- or four-course meals to over 250 people every Sunday.

The organization, in London, is a registered charity which was started in 1988. It's staffed by volunteers who make up teams of kitchen helpers, cooks, drivers and navigators, who regularly give up a few hours each month to cook and deliver the meals. They prepare the finest meats, fruits and vegetables on Sunday mornings in five kitchens around the capital.

In consultation with a dietician, each meal is designed to provide the maximum in nourishment and taste. They are also happy to meet any special diet, be it based on medical grounds or ethical/personal preferences. This might mean cooking diabetic, gluten-free or vegetarian/vegan alternatives.

The meals are swiftly packed in hot boxes and transported in private cars to Food Chain service users. Special delivery routes have been devised to make sure everyone receives their meal fresh and hot.

Here are two examples of Food Chain menus, prepared and devised by one of their cooks, Victoria Berman.

These recipes are some of the ones I've found most successful for a variety of reasons. Firstly, I think they taste good and look good. They're very colourful and hence appetizing, especially when served with contrasting or complementary colours in side vegetables, salad or rice. They take a minimum of preparation time (important if you're not sure how many people will turn up to help you!) and they travel reasonably well.

VICTORIA BERMAN'S FOOD CHAIN MENUS

Menu 1

Carrot and Coriander Soup (v)
Serves 4

Ingredients
2 oz onions, finely chopped
½ oz butter
½ lb carrots peeled and chopped
1 heaped teaspoon coriander, finely chopped
salt and pepper
1 tablespoon crème fraîche
½ pint water

Method
Fry the onions in butter gently until softened. Add the carrots, coriander, salt and pepper to taste and about ½ pint of water. Bring to the boil and simmer gently for about 25 minutes, covered. Allow to cool, then liquidize the mixture.

To serve, reheat with crème fraîche.

Red Pepper Chicken
Serves 4

Ingredients
2 large red peppers
6 oz onions
1½ oz ground almonds
small piece fresh ginger
salt and pepper
olive oil
1 pint water
4 large or 6 small chicken breasts
2 tablespoons lemon juice

Method
Put the red peppers, onions, ground almonds, fresh ginger, salt and pepper into a food processor or blender to obtain a smooth paste. Heat the oil and fry the paste gently for about 10 minutes, be careful not to burn. Cut the chicken breasts into quarters and add to the pan with ½ a pint of water and the lemon juice and bring to the boil. Cover and simmer for 30 minutes stirring, once or twice.

Apple Pudding
serves 4

Ingredients
2 lb cooking apples
4 oz sugar
2 fl oz (or a bit more) milk
4 oz self-raising flour
1 teaspoon cinnamon
2 oz melted butter
2 large eggs

Method
Peel and core the apples, cut into chunks and line an ovenproof dish with them. Beat the sugar, milk and eggs together, then add flour and cinnamon. Stir in melted butter and pour over apples. Cook at Gas Mark 4 for 30–40 minutes.

Menu 2

Pasta and Feta Cheese Salad (v)
Serves 4

Ingredients
200 g pasta spirals
peppers: red, orange, yellow, green, ⅓ of each
100 g feta cheese, cubed
50 g black olives, stoned
20 ml lemon juice
1 teaspoon clear honey
1 teaspoon mustard
salt, pepper and olive oil

Method
Cook the pasta and allow to cool (you can mix with about 1 tablespoon of olive oil to stop the pasta sticking together). Slice the peppers lengthwise into thin strips and soften in a little oil for about 10 minutes (green peppers need a head start as they take a bit longer). Add to the pasta along with the feta cheese and olives. Make a dressing with the lemon juice, honey, mustard, salt and pepper, and mix well.

Citrus Coriander Lamb
Serves 4

Ingredients
2 lb lamb
2 tablespoons flour
2 tablespoons ground coriander
2 lb celeriac
2 bay leaves
1 teaspoon sugar
salt and pepper
olive oil
1 lemon
1 lime
1 large onion, chopped
1 pint water
½ lb leeks, sliced
½ lb parsnips, chopped
2 tablespoons fresh coriander

Method
Trim and cube the lamb and toss in a flour and ground coriander mixture. Peel the celeriac and cut into 1-inch cubes. Heat up 1–2 tablespoons oil and fry the celeriac for about 5 minutes until it's starting to brown. Cut the lemon and lime in half, then quarter the halves. Add to the celeriac in the pan and fry for another minute or so. Remove from the pan and keep warm. Add a little more oil to the pan and brown the onion and the lamb slightly. Add one pint of water, bay leaves, sugar, salt and pepper and half the fresh coriander and bring to the boil. Either simmer, covered, for 30

minutes or transfer to an ovenproof dish and cook, covered, at Gas Mark 4 for 30 minutes. Add the parsnips, leeks, celeriac and citrus and the rest of the fresh coriander and cook for a further 30 minutes.

Don't eat the lemon and lime pieces! (Although they won't harm you if you do.)

Chocolate Ginger Pear Tart
Serves 4

Ingredients
75 g digestive biscuits
75 g ginger biscuits
2 teaspoons cocoa powder
50 g butter
150 g cream cheese
2 teaspoons icing sugar
4 pear quarters (plus juice from the tin)
15 g plain chocolate

Method
Crush the biscuits and mix with the cocoa powder. Melt the butter and add to the biscuit mix. Stir well and either divide into four dishes or use a small cake tin. Press down firmly and chill for ½ hour or so. Mix the cream cheese with the sugar and 4 tablespoons of juice from the pear tin and spread evenly over the base. Melt the chocolate with 1 tablespoon of pear juice and cut the pear quarters into fans. Arrange the pear quarters on the top of the cheese mixture and decorate with chocolate.

The Food Chain is staffed by volunteers and relies on Charitable donations. Similar organizations exist across the States. If you can spare time to volunteer or give a donation, please contact:
The Food Chain, 25 Bertram Street, London N19 5DQ, tel 0171 272 2272, fax 0171 272 2273,
or one of the American organizations listed overleaf.

**AIDS meal service providers
throughout the United States:**

CALIFORNIA

Catholic Charities HIV Food
Services of San Mateo
600 Columbia Drive
San Mateo, CA 94402
(415) 579-0277, ext. 335

Helping Hands
1936 E. 4th St.
Long Beach, CA 90802
(310) 436-2614 fax

Laguna Shanti
Meals provided throughout
Orange City
401 Glenneyre, Ste. C
Laguna Beach, CA 92651
(714) 494-1446
(714) 497-2496 fax

Mama's Kitchen
1875 Second Avenue
San Diego, CA 92101
(619) 233-6262
(619) 233-6283 fax

Project Angel Food
7574 Sunset Boulevard
Los Angeles, CA 90046-3413
(213) 845-1800
http://www.angelfood.org

Project Open Hand
2720 17th St
San Francisco, CA 94115
(415) 558-0600

COLORADO
Project Angel Heart
915 E. 9th Ave
Denver, CO 80218
(303) 338-1315
(303) 830-1840 fax

FLORIDA
Cure AIDS Now, Inc.
111 SW 3rd St
Miami, FL 33130-1926
(305) 375-0400
(305) 375-8400 fax

GEORGIA
Project Open Hand
176 Ottley Dr., NE
Atlanta, GA 30324
(404) 872-8089 Admin
(404) 872-6947 Client Serv

ILLINOIS
Open Hand Chicago
909 West Belmont, Ste. 100
Chicago, IL 60657
(312) 665-1000
(312) 665-0044 fax

LOUISIANA
Food for Friends
2533 Columbus
New Orleans, LA 70119
(504) 944-6028
(504) 944-4441 fax

MARYLAND
Moveable Feast
P. O. Box 22248
Baltimore, MD 21203
(410) 243-4604 phone and fax

MASSACHUSETTS
Community Servings
125 Magazine St
Roxbury, MA 02119
(617) 445-7777
(617) 445-2444 fax

NEW MEXICO
Kitchen Angles
500 N Guadalupe, No. G505
Santa Fe, NM 87501
(505) 471-7780

NEW YORK

God's Love We Deliver
166 Avenue of the Americas
New York, NY 10013
(212) 294-8100
(212) 294-8101 fax

Meals on Wheels
(Rochester and Monroe Country)
2180 Empire Blvd
Webster, NY 14580
(716) 787-8397
(716) 787-9729 fax

OHIO

F.A.C.T., AIDS Task Force of
Greater Cleveland
2728 Euclid
Cleveland, OH 44115
(216) 621-0766
(216) 622-7785 fax

Project Open Hand
787 East Broad St
Columbus, OH 43205
(614) 221-5683
(614) 221-5633 fax
e-mail: pohc@aol.com

OREGON
HIV Center
Ecumenical Ministries of Oregon
3835 SW Kelly Ave
Portland, OR 97201
(503) 223-3444
(503) 223-3056 fax

PENNSYLVANIA
Manna
P. O. Box 30181
Philadelphia, PA 19103
(215) 496-2662
(215) 496-1349 fax

UTAH
Utah AIDS Foundation
(Services offered state-wide)
1408 S. 1100 E
Salt Lake City, UT 84105
(810) 487-2323/800-865-5004
in-state toll-free

WASHINGTON

Chicken Soup Brigade
1002 E. Senenca
Seattle, WA 98122
(206) 328-8979
(206) 328-0171 fax

WASHINGTON D. C.

Food & Friends
P. O. Box 70601
Washington, DC 20024
(202) 488-8278

Special Occasions

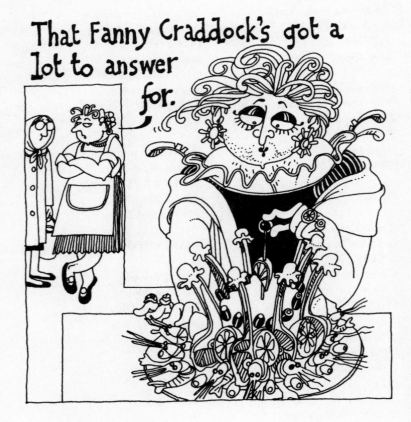

The Queer Christmas

The one meal that so typifies straightness can be completely invested with queerness. The best Christmas meals I've had have been queer ones. The meal is essential, as is the planning of the day and the selection of the guests. Because this is a queer Christmas it's not essential to stick to the traditional meal, but it is a goodie so I've outlined the basics.

Turkey

Think about the appetites of your guests before you buy: you can use the leftovers but they do become tedious after a couple of days. Fresh turkeys are best, but no one will really notice just so long as it's well defrosted. Clean the turkey, taking out all the giblets and messy stuff. If you're adventurous and want to make gravy out of the giblets then it's up you, but I'm far too squeamish and think Bisto and a bit of turkey juice will do. Take off the trussing and if you're into stuffing (I am), then stuff between the skin and breast, and in the neck.

Pre-heat your oven to Gas Mark 7. Rub butter all over the skin of the bird by turning it on its side and then on the other side. Roast the turkey on each side for 10 minutes and then turn the heat down to Gas Mark 4 and roast for 12 minutes per 1 lb – small birds may need slightly more. You can check it's done by putting a skewer into the leg to check for pink juices – there won't be any if it's done. Don't keep opening the oven, it'll screw up your timings.

Roast Potatoes et al.

I always blanch potatoes before roasting them – just boil them in salted water for five minutes, then add them to the oil in the roasting tin and roast for 35–45 minutes.

Carrots can be made more interesting if you add a couple of tablespoons of soy sauce and some roasted cumin seeds.

Parsnips can be roasted with the potatoes but the meal can end up somewhat greasy. I prefer to mash them (as you would potatoes).

Bread Sauce
Serves 8

Ingredients
1 pint milk
1 large onion, quartered
2 mace blades
ground mace
12 peppercorns
1 bay leaf
6 cloves
4 oz fresh white breadcrumbs
2 tablespoons double cream

Method

Place the milk, onion, mace, peppercorns, bay leaf, and cloves in a pan. Bring slowly to the boil and simmer for 5 minutes. Remove from the heat and stand for 2 hours.

Sieve the milk and return to the pan and stir in the breadcrumbs. Cook over a low heat stirring gently until the crumbs have swollen. Add the cream when it's time to serve.

Celeriac Mash
Serves 6 – 8 festive friends

An unusual side vegetable with a
great flavour.

Ingredients
2 lb celeriac, cut into cubes
3 cloves garlic
2 oz butter
100 ml milk
handful parsley, chopped

Method
Cook the celeriac in boiling salted
water with the garlic cloves for 10 –
15 minutes until tender. Drain and
place in a blender. Add the butter
and process, slowly adding milk to
make a velvety texture. Mix in the
parsley and serve.

Leek Gratin
Serves 6 leek-lovers

Ingredients
8 oz tomatoes
3 lb leeks
pinch salt
½ oz butter
1 shallot
1¼ cups thick double cream
pepper

Method
Skin the tomatoes and take out the
seeds, dice them. Wash and trim the
leeks, and peel and chop the shallot.
Bring 5 pints of water to the boil
with a pinch of salt. Blanch the leeks
for 8 minutes. Then plunge them in
iced water to prevent further cooking and dry them on kitchen towels
and cut them into 2 inch rings. Melt
the butter in a ovenproof dish and
cook the shallot gently until transparent. Remove the dish from the
heat and spread the diced tomato on
top of the shallot and the leeks on
top of them, grind some pepper over
them. Heat the cream and pour it
over the top.

Pop in a medium oven and bake for
15 minutes, serve immediately.

Baby Turnips stuffed with Mushroom
Serves 6

For those show-offs amongst us.

Ingredients
2 lbs small turnips with green tops
8 oz mushrooms
½ shallot
1 oz butter
1 cup double cream
2 large tomatoes
sprig of chervil

Method
Preheat a medium oven to Gas Mark 6. Peel the turnips leaving the stems intact, and place in a saucepan of cold water. Bring to the boil and blanch for 3 minutes and drain. Put the turnips on a buttered ovenproof dish, add water until the turnips are almost, but not totally covered. Sprinkle with salt, cover with foil and bake in the oven for 1½ hours until they're tender when pierced.

Meanwhile, wash and dry the mushrooms and chop them finely. Peel and finely chop the shallot. Melt the butter in a saucepan, add the shallot and cook until it's transparent. Add the mushrooms, salt and pepper. Mix thoroughly and cook gently, stirring until almost all the liquid has evaporated.

Tip
To skin the tomatoes you can pop them on a fork over a gas flame; when the skin blisters, quickly peel it off.

Bring the cream to the boil in a small pan. Boil until slighlty reduced and thickened. Skin, slice and seed the tomatoes. Remove the cooked turnips, drain and cut in half. Fill them with the mushroom mixture. Replace the tops and pour a pool of the hot cream on to each heated turnip. Garnish with the tomato slices and chervil sprigs.

Now serve with a satisfied grin, knowing that you've made more effort than any of your guests would have thought capable of you.

Mince Pies

Although you can spend hours creating your own mincemeat and slaving over your own pastry, it has to be said that the most simple way to make mince pies is to buy both the mincemeat and puff pastry. Just pop them in a medium oven for 20 minutes, reduce the heat and cook for a further 10 minutes. Easy and tasty.

Christmas Cake
Serves all your Yuletide guests

Ingredients
1½ lb mixed dried fruit
4 oz candied peel, chopped
8 oz glacé cherries
5 fl oz sherry or orange juice
9 oz plain wholewheat flour
and plain white flour, mixed
1 teaspoon baking powder
½ teaspoon mixed spice
¼ teaspoon freshly grated
nutmeg
9 oz butter or soft
vegetarian margarine
9 oz soft brown sugar
4 free-range eggs, lightly
beaten
grated rind of 1 orange
grated rind of 1 lemon
2 oz ground almonds
2 oz flaked almonds
2 tablespoons brandy

Method
Put the dried fruit into a bowl with the candied peel. Rinse and halve the cherries and add to the bowl, along with the sherry or orange juice. Mix, then cover and leave to marinate for 1–2 days, stirring occasionally.

Line a 20 cm/8 in round cake tin with a double layer of greaseproof paper, and tie a double layer of newspaper around the outside of the tin. Pre-heat the oven to Gas Mark 1. Sift together the flours, baking powder and spice. Cream the butter or margarine with the sugar, then beat in the eggs a little at a time. Fold in the flour mixture, then stir in the fruit, orange and lemon rinds, and the ground and flaked almonds.

Spoon the mixture into the prepared tin and bake for 4¼ hours, until a skewer inserted into the middle of the cake comes out clean. Stand the cake in its tin on a wire rack to cool.

Remove the cake from the tin and strip off the paper. Prick the cake all over with a skewer and pour over the brandy. Wrap in greaseproof paper and store in an airtight tin until required. The cake will keep well for 1–3 months and mature during that time. Sprinkle with a little more brandy during storage. Cover with marzipan, then royal icing or sugar paste.

Christmas Pudding

Makes 2 x 3 lb puddings

Some queers have masochistic tendencies, it's true. If you happen to be one of those people, then this recipe is for you. I personally would rather spend five minutes in Sainsbury's, but if you want to slave over an oven for days to get either sympathy or sexual favours, it's up to you. And here's how to do it.

Ingredients

8 oz self-raising flour

6 oz fresh coarse breadcrumbs

3½ oz ground almonds

½ oz ground mixed spice

1 lb muscovado sugar

1 teaspoon nutmeg

¼ teaspoon ground cloves

14 oz unsalted butter, chopped

1 large orange

1 small lemon

1 lime

¼ pint Guinness

6 tablespoons dark rum

7 oz cut mixed peel

12 oz prunes, chopped roughly

8 oz sultanas or seedless raisins

8 oz currants

8 oz grated apple

4 eggs, beaten

1 tablespoon brandy

Method

Mix together the dry ingredients and rub in the butter. Wash and quarter the orange, lemon and lime. Remove the pips and purée the fruits with their skins still on. Stir them into the dry ingredients, then stir in the remaining ingredients except the eggs. Cover and leave for a day or so, stirring occasionally. When you've decided to actually cook the thing, add in the eggs. Fill the pudding basins to ⅔ full. Cover the top of the basins with greaseproof paper and tie with string. Place in a saucepan and pour in boiling water to halfway up the basins. Put a lid on the saucepans and simmer for six hours, checking that the water doesn't dry out. The puddings can be stored for up to three months.

When you serve the puds, pour over some brandy and set light – but be careful not to incinerate your hair, tablecloth, guests, etc.

The Alternative Veggie-Gourmet Queer Christmas Meal

For when we've decided to make an effort and spend the entire day luxuriating in supremely delightful vegetarian offerings.

Walnut Tartlets with a Wild Mushroom and Leek Goulash draped in Red Pepper Sauce

Serves 6

Ingredients

Pastry:
6 oz medium oatmeal
3 oz ground walnuts
½ teaspoon ground cumin
1 teaspoon dried thyme
water, to mix

Goulash:
1 tablespoon extra virgin olive oil
1 clove garlic, crushed
4 medium leeks, thinly sliced
1 lb wild mushrooms (including oyster or shiitake)
2 tablespoons tomato purée
1 tablespoon paprika
black pepper

Method

Mix the oatmeal, walnuts and seasonings. Add enough water to form a fairly sticky dough. Press out into tartlet cases. Bake blind for 15 minutes at Gas Mark 6 until they're golden. Then heat the oil with a little water, add the garlic and leeks. Sweat them for about 5 minutes, add the sliced mushrooms, starting with the firmest, and sauté until tender, adding more water if necessary. Then add the tomato purée, paprika and pepper and heat through. Pour into cooked flan cases and garnish with toasted pepper strips and toasted walnuts.

Red Pepper Sauce:

2 large red peppers, roughly chopped

2 garlic cloves, roughly chopped

pinch cayenne pepper

¼ pint water

2 tablespoons extra virgin olive oil

Black pepper

For the sauce, simmer the peppers, garlic and cayenne in a little water until they're tender, then liquidize them and dribble in the olive oil. Add pepper to taste and reheat to coincide with the spectacular serving of the tartlets.

Cashew and Caper Loaf

Well it is Christmas and we do like all the veggies so this is a very good way to have the pomp and ceremony of the meal without the meat.

Ingredients

½ pint milk

1 large onion, chopped

2 bay leaves

6 peppercorns

1 heaped teaspoon cornflour

8 oz millet, cooked (save this for the birds!)

6 oz ground cashew nuts

pepper

2 oz capers, soaked in fresh water and drained

grated nutmeg

Method

Put the milk in a pan with the onion, bay leaves and peppercorns. Bring to the boil and leave covered for 20 minutes. Strain the bay leaves and peppercorns out of the pan. Separately, mix the cornflour with enough milk to make a smooth paste and add to the remaining milk in a pan, bring to the boil and simmer until it's thick. Add the sauce to the millet, onion, cashews and seasonings, then fold in the capers. Place in a greased loaf tin and bake at Gas Mark 5 for 45 minutes until it's firm and golden.

Tip

You need good sauces for nut loaves, not just gravy and bread sauce. I think the ideal sauce for this would be Maria Esposito's Pasta Sauce with some extra herbal infusion.

Nutty Vegetable Loaf

Another Christmas loaf, this one's less distinctive than the last one but probably more generally pleasing to a large crowd.

Ingredients

1 onion, finely chopped

½ red pepper, finely chopped

1 medium baking apple, grated

2 oz finely ground nuts – almonds, hazelnuts, etc.

1 dessertspoon tomato purée

½ teaspoon cayenne pepper

¼ teaspoon thyme

½ level teaspoon mustard (optional)

1 dessertspoon olive oil

1 medium carrot, grated

4 oz cooked brown rice

¼ teaspoon mace

black pepper

¼ teaspoon rosemary

Method

Sauté the onion and pepper in the oil until they soften and begin to brown. Add the grated carrot and apple and fry for another two minutes. Add the remaining ingredients and mix well. Place the mixture into a greased loaf tin and bake for approximately 40 minutes at Gas Mark 6.

Tip

Some people have dangerous allergies to nuts, so beware.

Tips for the Best Queer Christmas

• Make the effort – often Christmases can be sadly reminiscent of the cheesy yules of our youths and typify why we're not with them.

• Booze, booze, booze: start with gin and tonics, then on to the white and then red, and then port with your cheese. Then you can settle down to some serious game playing.

• Presentation is key. Crackers may seem overly heterosexual but there's nothing more heartening than to see your guests having serious conversations sporting stupid paper hats.

• Games are essential: charades, the famous people game (everyone writes the names of ten famous people on pieces of paper and puts them in a hat. The guests form pairs and read clues out to each other against the clock), and, when you're drunk, the truth games start with the revelations that you all dislike/like/fancy each other, and always have.

• The best way to cope with the present situation is to ask all your guests to buy a present to the value of £5 or £10 and then distribute them anonymously.

• Don't think you can do all this on your own, demand booze and cheeses from your guests.

Weird Easter

Tina's Greek Entrail Easter Soup
Serves 4 – 6

This is a special Easter dish that people eat after coming back from Midnight Mass on Easter Saturday. In Greece people don't eat meat or oil during Lent, so on Easter Saturday they literally eat their guts out. It's a heavy soup made from lamb entrails. Because meat is seen as being expensive, many people rear their own lambs and use the whole lamb to make it last. There's also mythology connected with entrails making you potent. It's very sexy food but most people avoid it because it's so ghoulish – I think it's very queer.

In order to find the entrails you have to go to either a Greek or a Turkish butcher. The entrails basically consist of everything from the neck down apart from the stomach (we reserve that for tripe), so it's liver, heart, lungs, kidneys, spleen and sweetbreads (glands) which are absolutely delicious. The original entrail soup also includes intestines but I've been unable to get hold of these in the UK.

Ingredients

1 medium lamb's entrails
(well over 1 kg)

large onion, chopped

4 tablespoons butter
or olive oil

2 teaspoons dill

1 vegetable stock cube

1 bunch spring onions
chopped

juice of 2 lemons

2–3 eggs

salt and pepper

50 g rice per person

Method

Boil the entrails until the foam
comes out of them and clarify by
spooning off the foam from the pan.
Remove from the pan and cut into
small cubes (1 inch). Sauté the
onion in the butter and add the
entrails and dill, salt and pepper.
When they're browned a bit, add
the stock cube diluted in a pint of
water and let them boil. Add the
rice to the boiling mixture (adding
extra water if needs be to keep the
soup thick). When the rice is cooked
the meat should be also (about ½ an
hour). Beat the eggs and add the
lemon juice. Take 2 ladles of juice
out of the entrail pan and add slowly
to the eggs (to avoid curdling). Then
add the egg mixture to the soup.

Serve with bread and red or white
wine. In Greece they serve it with
hard-boiled eggs on the side.

I have served it before in this country and nobody would touch it, as
they noticed that the pieces of meat
were unidentifiable and a bit rub-
bery (especially the lungs). But it is
gorgeous, I assure you.

Hot Cross Buns
Makes 12 buns

Ingredients

½ pint (300 ml) milk, plus extra to glaze

4 oz caster sugar

½ oz dried yeast

1lb strong bread flour

1 level teaspoon salt

pinch mixed spice

pinch cinnamon

pinch nutmeg

4 oz currants

1 oz mixed chopped peel

1 egg, beaten

1 oz butter, melted

flour, for the work surface

shortcrust pastry trimmings

Method

Heat the milk to lukewarm and pour into a pint measure. Add a level teaspoon caster sugar and the yeast and whisk with a fork; leave for about 5 to 10 minutes until frothy. Sift the flour with the salt and spices into a large bowl. Add 2 oz caster sugar and the fruit. Stir the egg and butter into the yeast mixture, add the flour and mix well. This will make a soft dough.

Turn the dough onto a floured table and knead for about 10 minutes until smooth and no longer sticky. Place in a lightly oiled polythene bag and leave to rise at room temperature for 1½ hours or until double in bulk. Divide the dough into 12 pieces and shape into buns by using the palm of your hand, pressing down hard and then easing up. Place well spaced on a floured baking sheet. Put inside the oiled polythene bag and leave to rise at room temperature for about 1 hour until doubled in bulk. Remove the bag. Roll out the pastry trimmings and cut into 24 strips about 4 in long and put two strips in a cross on each bun dampening the underside with water to make them stick. Bake in a hot oven (Gas Mark 7) for 15 – 20 minutes until golden brown.

Make a glaze by bringing 2 tablespoons water and 2 tablespoons milk
to the boil, stirring in 1½ oz caster
sugar and then boiling for 2 minutes.
Remove the buns from the oven and
glaze at once.

Steve's 'Lazy Queen'
July 4th/Super Bowl Party

Serves as many queens as you can accommodate

Hamburgers

Use lean non-British beef, 1 – 2 burgers per guest.

Toppings:
Tomato sauce, mustard (Dijon for pretentious friends), cheese, lettuce, sliced tomatoes, mayonnaise

Hot Dogs

1-2 per guest

Toppings:
Mustard, chopped onions, coleslaw, pickle relish, chili sauce (a mildly spicy mince, without beans)

(Optional fare: Bar-B-Q Chicken, Veggie Burgers)

Hamburger/Hot Dog buns should be steamed or may be toasted, however many people use them right from the bag - if so, be sure they're fresh.

Baked Beans

Mix with a little mustard and brown sugar, bake until the top edges become crusty, one 'lasagna pan' per dozen guests (absolute must if you're in the Boston area).

Cole Slaw

With good varieties available in the delicatessens these days, it's not worth the hassles and scraped knuckles to make it yourself. Figure roughly 100g per guest, some people won't touch the stuff.

Crisps

Plain, salted potato 'chips' with French Onion dip were always the standard before many different flavours became available, as well as a wide variety of dips (have several large bags available but open only as needed – remaining bags can be devoured during future episodes of 'Neighbours').

Ice Cream

Requirement for July 4th as it's usually pretty hot in most parts of America for this event. For the Super Bowl many people have a large decorated sheet cake on hand, appropriate to the teams playing that year – to avoid confrontation, decorate with BOTH teams playing.

Beverages

Plenty of soft drinks and cold beer: Coke, Diet Coke (Caffeine Free Diet Coke for hyper-active friends); it is also good to have fruit juice and/or bottled water on hand. Budweiser and Miller are the classic American beers for this type of event – use Bud Lite and Miller Lite for figure conscious queens. Plastic coolers and large rubbish bins can come in handy here, fill them with layers of ice and drinks and alow guests to serve themselves. Quantity? You know your friends better than I do, sweetheart.

Tips

Garnish EVERYTHING using toothpicks with little paper American flags. Make it easy on yourself, there are plenty of novelty items available such as 'red, white & blue' paper plates, cups, table covers and serviettes to use for serving.

If friends offer to bring anything, say 'Yes!'.

If you're lucky enough that most of your friends are rugby players, treble all serving suggestions.

Party Food

Party Tips

• Give people plenty of advance notice so that they have no excuses. I suggest sending invites for Christmas parties mid-November.

• Over-invite (but always try to steer clear of people you actually really dislike).

• Decide on the scale of your party well in advance. A small gathering is hugely different to a massive bash and the in-between area is often unsatisfactory.

• Don't invite your ex(es) or anyone else's.
• Buy loads of alcohol – cheap bottles of Bulgarian Sauvignon and those tiny bottles of supermarket lager are a good bet.
• Sort out your music and have back-ups, should someone decide to stamp on your amplifier in a fit of pique.
• Hide a proportion of your alcohol in those 'hard-to-find' places. I recommend laundry baskets, wardrobes and airing cupboards (although your well-stashed lager could become a little tepid).
• Produce food in bulk. Bread's always a winner, as are pasta salad, potato salad and crudités.
• It's obvious but remove all breakables, family heirlooms, Turkish rugs and valuable records.
• Although a 'mix' is always successful, don't go mad. Your 'liberal' aunt may find the sight of a fisting threesome rather alarming.
• Be specific about timing. If you go for, say, 9.45p.m., people may actually show up on time thinking that there's some sort of cabaret – which of course there won't be.

Themed parties are an excellent idea as long as you can guarantee that a decent number of guests will make the effort. Keep the theme broad and affordable.

Themes to avoid:
    Shakespearian (too fancy)
    Star Trek (too nerdy and may put off anyone with a personality)
    Famous Sondheim musicals (you'll put off the dykes)
    Toga (too juvenile and irritating, will only attract morons)

Themes to encourage:
    '70s (always fun to see your friends in flares and ponchos)
    Colours (no excuse not to – unless it's beige)
    Murder (always a winner)

• If any of your guests have taken amphetamines, they may possibly be persuaded to indulge in a frantic cleaning spree at 5a.m. when all the potential dull conversation has been exhausted.
• Toilet paper in bulk is essential.
• Keep a check on your bedroom, you never know who could be taking refuge in it.
• Punch is a good way to disguise cheap alcohol, as is mulled wine.
• Don't be tempted by line-dancing – it's inherently naff.

Curry Lentil Pâté (v)

Health, health, health (and actually tastes pretty good).

Ingredients
4 oz red lentils
8 fl oz water
1 bay leaf
1 tablespoon sunflower oil
4 oz onion, finely chopped
½ teaspoon ground turmeric
½ teaspoon ground cumin
6 oz carrot, finely grated
black pepper
1 tablespoon natural yoghurt
coriander leaves, to garnish

Method

Put the lentils in the water in a saucepan with the bay leaf. Put a lid on and bring to the boil. Simmer for 35–40 minutes until the lentils are soft. Remove from the heat, take out the bay leaf and mash to a purée (or pop in a blender for a minute). In a separate pan (or the same one after a quick wash), heat the oil and cook the onion over a low heat for two minutes, then add the spices and grated carrot and cook for a further two minutes. Stir in the cooked lentils and season with black pepper. Allow to cool before stirring in the yoghurt. Divide the mixture into four baked-egg dishes and garnish with coriander leaves.

Sunflower Tartlets (v)
Makes 12

Ingredients

Pastry
4 oz plain wholemeal flour
2 oz margarine
Cold water, to mix

Filling
2 teaspoons sunflower oil
2 oz onion, finely chopped
½ green pepper, de-seeded and chopped
4 tablespoons sweetcorn
1 egg
3 tablespoons skimmed milk
black pepper
½ oz Cheddar cheese, grated
3 teaspoons sunflower seeds

Method

Put the flour in a bowl and rub the margarine in until the mixture resembles fine breadcrumbs. Chill for 10–15 minutes and then add just enough water to make a soft dough. Roll out the dough to a rectangle and cut out rounds with a pastry cutter to line 12 greased small tart tins. Carefully press the pastry into the tins and bake blind for 5 minutes. Prepare the filling. Heat the oil in a saucepan and cook the onion and pepper for a few minutes over a low heat. Stir in the sweetcorn kernels and continue to cook for 2 minutes. Beat the egg with the milk and season with black pepper to taste. Divide the onion mixture between the tarts, spoon a little egg and milk mixture over the top and sprinkle grated cheese and sunflower seeds on top. Bake for 10–12 minutes until the filling is set and brown. Serve cold.

Hummus (v)

I'm a particularly lazy cook and tend to pop down to Sainsburys to purchase my hummus but should you want to really impress your guests, this is how you make it.

Ingredients
8 oz chickpeas
(soaked overnight)
5 cloves garlic
6 tablespoons tahini
large pinch paprika
1 teaspoon ground cumin
8–10 tablespoons cold water
juice of 1 lemon
freshly ground black pepper

Method

Drain the chickpeas and put in a saucepan. Add plenty of boiling water to cover the pulses by about two inches. Cover and boil for two hours or until tender. Drain. Put the chickpeas in a blender with the remaining ingredients and blend until it's a purée (add water acording to your taste).

Ingredients
8 oz cream cheese
8 oz mature Cheddar, grated
2 oz butter
1 teaspoon Worcestershire
  sauce
dash Tabasco sauce

Potted Cheese (v)

Method

Just whack it all in the blender and away we go.

Blue Cheese Dip (v)

Ingredients
¼ lb blue cheese
1 tablespoon chopped
fresh chives
4 tablespoons sour cream
few drops Tabasco sauce
pinch nutmeg
pepper

Method
Place the ingredients in a blender
and Bob's your uncle.

Rick Richardson's Melon Salsa (v)

Ingredients
1 cup cantaloupe melon
1 cup honeydew melon
1 cup watermelon
1 cup jicama
1 small red onion
1 cup parsley
1 jalepeño pepper (seeded)
juice of 1 lime
salt and pepper, to taste

Method
Cut up the melons and jicima in ½-
inch cubes. Chop the onion. Dice
the parsley and jalepeño (finely).
Add lime juice and salt and pepper.
Toss everything together and call it
salad.

It's better if it's marinated overnight
in the refridgerator.

F e l a f e l   (v)
Serves 4

Ingredients

½ lb chickpeas (soaked overnight and cooked for 1½ hours

2 cloves garlic, peeled and chopped finely

1 onion, grated

1 oz fresh coriander leaves

1 teaspoon ground cumin

1 teaspoon ground coriander

½ teaspoon cayenne

½ teaspoon turmeric

½ teaspoon baking powder

1 egg, beaten lightly

juice of ½ lemon

flour

8 tablespoons sunflower oil

M e t h o d

Blend the chickpeas in a food-processor until they form a smooth paste. Add the garlic, onion, coriander leaves, ground cumin, ground coriander, cayenne, turmeric, baking powder, egg and lemon juice, and blend again. Leave to stand for 30 minutes. Shape the mixture into small round balls (2½ inches deep), adding a little flour and water if they are not binding.

Heat the oil in a frying pan over a medium heat and fry the felafel until golden brown, turning over after a few minutes.

Serve with hummus and pitta bread.

P o t a t o   S a l a d   (v)
Serves 4

Ingredients

2 lb small new potatoes

3 tablespoons olive oil

1 tablespoon wine vinegar

1 teaspoon salt

1 teaspoon black pepper

2 oz chives (chopped) or 3 spring onions, finely chopped

M e t h o d

Scrub the potatoes and put them in a saucepan, cover it with water and bring to the boil. Simmer for 12–15 minutes. Drain the potatoes, chop them into larkish, bite-sized chunks and place in a bowl. Add the oil, vinegar, salt and pepper, and mix lightly, then leave to cool. Add the chives or spring onions just before serving the salad.

Tuna Pâté

Ingredients
8 oz canned tuna, drained
4 oz soft butter
salt and pepper
lemon juice to taste
small bunch of dill

Method
It's blender time again, and this is
simple and smooth.

Scotch Eggs
Makes 4–6

Ingredients
8 oz sausage meat
1 teaspoon Worcestershire
sauce
1 tablespoon chopped parsley
1 teaspoon dried mixed herbs
salt and pepper
2 teaspoons Dijon mustard
1 tablespoon plain flour
4 eggs, hard-boiled
1 egg, beaten
dried breadcrumbs
oil for deep-frying

Method
Put the sausage meat in a bowl. Stir
in the Worcestershire sauce and
herbs, and season with salt and pepper. Divide the mixture into four
portions and form each into a flat
cake. Spread with mustard.

Season the flour with salt and pepper and use to coat the eggs. Press
the sausage meat evenly around the
eggs, making sure there are no
cracks in the surface. Dip in the
beaten egg and breadcrumbs. Heat
the oil and deep-fry the eggs for 7 –
8 minutes until golden brown and
crisp. Drain on kitchen paper to
remove oil and leave to cool.

You can use vegetarian sausage
meat if you're feeling particularly
worthy. ·

Queer Cocktails

The quintessential queer beverage is a cocktail; from screwdrivers up there's nothing more impressive than a well-made and extremely well-presented alcoholic beverage. Straights have punch, we have cocktails.

Cocktail Tips:

• Use a shaker, it's worth the investment
• Shake vigorously whilst maintaining direct eye-contact with the future consumer
• Umbrellas are always a must
• Colours are important, as bright and vivid as possible

Cocktails are made by trial and error, a slurp here, a twist there, the only major thing that differentiates them is that some are long and some are short, so the ones marked 'cocktail' are the short ones and the glasses should be adjusted accordingly. The following drinks are just a few basics, tweaking can be implemented once the basics are there.

Alexander (cocktail)

3 parts Cognac
3 parts Brown Cacao
3 parts cream
Shake vigorously.

Americana (long drink)

1 centilitre Bourbon
2 centilitres champagne
2 drops of bitters
Garnish with a slice of peach.
Serve over ice.

B-52 (cocktail)

2 centilitres Kahlua
2 centilitres Bailey's
2 centilitres Cointreau
Layer the liqueurs in the order mentioned. Serve with a short straw and then set fire to the Cointreau.

Gin Thing (long drink)

2 centilitres dry gin
dash grenadine
1 centilitre freshly squeezed grapefruit juice
Mix all the ingredients over ice and drink immediately!

Black Russian (cocktail)
4 centilitres vodka
2 centilitres Kahlua

or use the common:
3 centilitres vodka
3 centilitres Kahlua
(For the one with a faint heart).

Blackberry Tequila (cocktail)
4 centilitres tequila
2 centilitres Crème de Cassis
1 lemon
Shake.

Blue Lady (cocktail)
4 centilitres gin
2 centilitres blue curaçao
2 lemons, squeezed
Shake.

Brave Bull (cocktail)
3 centilitres tequila
3 centilitres Kahlua
Stir.

Daiquiri (cocktail)
6 centilitres white rum
juice of 2 limes
1 teaspoon sugar
Shake.

Dry Martini (cocktail)
5 centilitres gin
1 centilitre Martini Extra Dry
Stir with ice and add a green
olive to each glass.

Earthquake (cocktail)
4 parts whisky
1 part gin
1 part Pernod
Shake.

Fire Bomb
1 part tequila
1 part Jack Daniels
1 part vodka
Few drops of Tabasco
I love the 'lady' cocktails, so ludi-
crously archaic I find them rather
cute but for the 'sensitive', lady
can be changed to 'amazon'.

Broomstick (cocktail)
1 part Drambuie
1 part Cointreau
1 part Amaretto
1 part Marsala wine
crushed ice
2 parts sweetened whipped
cream
Indian Tonic to fill
a very little nutmeg
Mix the Drambuie, Cointreau,
Amaretto and Marsala with the
crushed ice in a cocktail shaker.
Add the cream and mix it carefully with a bar spoon. Now add
a little tonic and very gently
shake the mixture – if you don't
it will curdle. Now pour the
mixture in a large, long drink
glass and fill up GENTLY with
the rest of the tonic. Sprinkle a
little nutmeg on top.

Irish Lady (cocktail)
4 centilitres Jamesons
(Irish whisky)
2 centilitres green curaçao
2 lemons, squeezed
Shake.

Ladies Lips (cocktail)
1 part Malibu
1 part grenadine
1 part Bailey's
1 part condensed milk
Shake.

Long-Island Ice Tea (long drink)
2 parts vodka
2 parts gin
2 parts rum
2 parts tequila
2 parts Triple Sec
Coke
Add Coke until the colour
is noticeable.

Lubricator (cocktail)
punnet of frozen strawberries
2 apples
boiling water
lemon vodka
Put 8–10 frozen strawberries in
the blender with half a cup of
boiling water .... leave to stand
while doing the next bit. Use a
juicer to extract the juice from
the apples. Then sieve the result
to give only the clearest juice.
Tip this into the blender. Put in
lemon vodka to taste (I usually
use about four shots). Blend and
then serve.

Maiden's Dream (cocktail)
3 parts Gin
3 parts Pernod
1 parts Grenadine
Stir.

Manhattan (cocktail)
4 centilitres whisky
2 centilitres Martini Bianco
1 drop Angostura Bitters
Stir.

Pina Colada (long drink)
6 parts rum
2 drops Angostura Bitters
1 part coconut milk
orange juice
Shake rum, Angostura Bitters
and coconut milk together. Add
orange juice.

Tom Collins (long drink)
6 centilitres gin
juice of 2 lemons
1 tablespoon sugar
tonic water
Stir together gin, lemon juice
and sugar, then add tonic water.